Neighbours

Josephine Monroe

Neighbours

THE FIRST 10 YEARS

Michael Joseph
London

MICHAEL JOSEPH LTD

Published by the Penguin Group
27 Wrights Lane, London W8 5TZ
Viking Penguin Inc., 375 Hudson Street, New York, New York 10014, USA
Penguin Books Australia Ltd, Ringwood, Victoria, Australia
Penguin Books Canada Ltd, 10 Alcorn Avenue, Toronto, Ontario, Canada M4V 3B2
Penguin Books (NZ) Ltd, 182-190 Wairau Road, Auckland 10, New Zealand

Penguin Books Ltd, Registered Offices: Harmondsworth, Middlesex, England

First published 1996
1 3 5 7 9 10 8 6 4 2

Printed in England by Butler & Tanner, Frome, Somerset

A CIP catalogue record for this book is available from the British Library

ISBN 0 7181 4212 8
The moral right of the author has been asserted

C O N T E N T S

TEN YEARS OF Neighbours

Introduction by Anne Haddy

This book has been published to celebrate the first ten years of *Neighbours* and I'd like to tell you a bit about the show and what it's been like to have been part of those ten years, playing Helen Daniels.

I started my career in Adelaide, South Australia, just after I left school. That was way back in 1948. There were no drama schools in Australia at that time, but various people taught drama. I studied with quite a few of them and began working in radio and the theatre. Never in my wildest dreams did I imagine that I would be cast in a long-running television show that is so successful and which I love doing.

I remember how I first came to be cast as Helen Daniels. I had had some heart trouble in 1979 which unfortunately set me back a bit. I was having dinner with a dear friend of mine, Colleen Clifford, in the Opera House between shows, and she happened to mention a film she was just about to make. I said 'I'd love to do a film,' and she said 'But my dear, you wouldn't be bankable' because of my dicky heart. She was eighty-five at the time!

Fortunately, Grundy Television didn't agree and asked me if I would be prepared to move down to Melbourne to play a character called Helen Daniels in a new serial called *Neighbours*. It would make a great change in my life; leaving my children and all my friends, as we lived in Sydney. My husband, being an actor, didn't require much persuasion – at that time neither of us was tied up. So here we are down in Melbourne enjoying it very much. Of course, Erinsborough is not in Melbourne specifically, but is any town in Australia.

On 2 January 1985, armed with scripts, I started the very first day of rehearsal. I thought the show might run for about two years, and it was a very sad day for all of us when we were axed after six months at Channel Seven.

We were so fortunate when Channel Ten picked up the show and we have been there ever since. Thank you Channel Ten and Grundy very much. There was very little change in the cast; we lost a couple and gained, among others, Anne Charleston, who played Madge Mitchell. At last I had a kindred spirit: a good actress, great to work with and we had many mutual friends.

Kylie Minogue and Jason Donovan also joined us then. They were so adored by the audiences, especially the young ones. Our ratings soared because people from all age groups loved *Neighbours*. After all those years in theatre and radio I was a 'star' overnight. At least, that's how I was referred to by the media. I wish I felt like one!

Then, lo and behold, my husband, James Condon, was cast as a chap called Douglas

Blake – not a very reputable bloke at all. So many people ask me what it's like working with my husband. We had done a bit of work together already, so Jim's being cast in *Neighbours* was another wonderful experience which we enjoyed tremendously. This Blake fellow was truly awful; he took all Helen's money – by devious means, naturally. One day, when Jim and I were out shopping, a woman came up to me and asked how I could bear to be with this terrible man. I had to tell her that he was my husband and that I loved him very much. She then rushed off, no doubt feeling rather foolish!

Unfortunately, Blake soon disappeared off the scene, but he did return a little later and Helen, thanks to Madge, got her money back. After many years Jim was cast as another character called Reuben White. He and Helen married and were very much in love, looking forward to an idyllic life together, but he had a heart attack and died. Poor old Helen.

So many of our good actors have been cast in *Neighbours* over the years. Fortunately, the majority of them have been teamed with me. I never get bored and I enjoy what I do tremendously. I must admit that it is difficult to remember everyone's name when they only pop in for a short time, but there is always 'darling' to fall back on when in doubt!

The days can be very long or very short, depending on the schedule, but every day is different, which, of course, means learning a new set of lines each weekend. Our directors are great people and they have a monthly turnaround. In fact, everyone who works on the show works with a love for the product, which makes for happy days in the studio.

When we had been working on the show for at least a couple of years the BBC bought it and, fortunately, *Neighbours* is very successful in the United Kingdom. So much so that I have many friends in England, Scotland, Wales and Ireland. I have had some marvellous presents from a few of them, which I cherish, and I receive many letters which I answer individually when I have the time. It is also quite surprising how many people have come out to live in Australia since watching *Neighbours* – even my General Practitioner! In 1988 I was made an Honorary Member of the Corpus Christi Junior Common Room at Oxford. Jim and I were in England that year and we were invited there by the students; I enjoyed that very much too.

The one event I remember above all others from my ten years in *Neighbours* happened one day when, as Helen, I was ushering people out of the front door of the Robinson's house. When it was my turn to go out I shut the door on my middle finger. I wrenched my finger out from between the door and the frame and held on to my bloody hand, waiting for someone to yell 'cut'. It seemed like an eternity before I heard the magic word and let out an almighty scream! Fortunately, the scene was all right so it didn't have to be shot again. I went down to the doctor who put four stitches in my hand and then back to the studio to finish my scenes for the day with my left hand behind my back!

Another thing that had me in stitches was when I asked for a peephole to be put in the front door. It was finally put in but when I went to look through it, it was far too high up for me to see through. I just went to pieces; never have I laughed so much. It's not so funny in the telling, but production was held up for quite a while.

All I can say now is thank you for watching *Neighbours* and for this book celebrating the first ten years.

My love to you all

ANNE HADDY

INTRODUCTION

Neighbours first came to our screens ten years ago, and the show has become so much a part of our everyday routines that it's hard to imagine ever having been without it. The humorous storylines, good-looking cast and friendly characters have made the programme a favourite with kids and students as well as everyone else in the family. And of course it's not just the Brits who love it – as well as Australia and Britain, *Neighbours* can be seen in nearly fifty countries all over the world, making it Australia's most successful soap ever.

But it wasn't always high ratings figures and international acclaim for the Ramsay Street soap – in the early days it was touch and go and it looked like *Neighbours* might not make its first birthday – never mind its tenth! The winning formula was dreamt up by Reg Watson, who had a track record for working on successful soaps both Down Under and in the UK. His recipe was as simple as can be: it was just three very different families – The Ramsays, The Robinsons and The Clarkes – living in the same street. But it was actually too simple, and Reg ended up writing twenty drafts of the first script in a bid to get the balance between humour and drama, friendliness and rivalry just right.

The next problem was finding a street to film in, and when a location scout spotted a cul-de-sac in a suburb of Melbourne not far from the studios, the makers of *Neighbours* knew they had found Ramsay Street. They asked each of the owners of the houses in the street if they would mind a few months' inconvenience, as no one expected *Neighbours* to last for very long. And now not only do the owners of those houses still have camera crews in their front gardens every week – but they also have tourists from all over the world coming to have a look!

When it came to casting the residents of Ramsay Street, the producers picked a mix of well-known faces – Alan Dale, Anne Haddy – and fresh-faced newcomers – Elaine Smith, David Clencie – and on 18 March 1985, Australians got their first look at their new neighbours.

But when the ratings failed to pick up, Channel Seven, who broadcast the soap, pulled the plug after just 170 episodes. The cast and crew expected to be laid off, and they would have been if it hadn't been for one man who worked for Grundy, the company that makes *Neighbours*. Ian Holmes believed in the show and the characters so much that he refused to let *Neighbours* die; he called rival broadcaster Channel Ten and offered the show to them. And when they agreed to air it, *Neighbours* became the first television drama in Australian history to be dumped by one station and then picked up by another.

Grundy's used the opportunity to fine-tune the show, axing some of the characters that weren't working out and introducing some new, younger characters including Mike, Clive and Charlene. But even with a new timeslot and an expensive advertising campaign, *Neighbours* still failed to bring in the viewers. The problem was that people in Australia's biggest city, Sydney, weren't tuning in. Traditionally, there has always been rivalry between Sydney and Melbourne, the city where *Neighbours* is made, and Sydneysiders didn't want to watch a soap from a rival city. So Channel Ten spent $500,000 promoting the show in Sydney by flying the cast there every weekend to make personal appearances and meet the public. They also sponsored a 'Neighbour of the Year' competition with the winner receiving a colour TV – to watch *Neighbours* on of course! It worked, and the viewing figures started to climb, but they still couldn't have predicted how successful the show would be abroad.

Neighbours was bought by the BBC to revamp their daytime schedule and the soap was first shown in the UK on 27 October 1986, and even though it was only aired in the morning and at lunch times, it still attracted a loyal audience. During the school holidays the figures swelled as schoolkids got hooked on the light-hearted mix of harmless pranks, mini crises and five minute romances. And when the school holidays finished, thousands of students still watched in their lunch hours or even skipped school to see key episodes! It was one pupil in particular who brought this trend to the attention of the BBC: Alison Grade, the daughter of the BBC's boss at the time, Michael Grade, and he ordered that *Neighbours* should get a post-school timeslot to catch the younger viewers. So the Aussie soap was moved to 5.35 p.m. where it has flourished ever since, attracting audiences of up to 15 million!

The huge success of *Neighbours* meant that canny theatre promoters and record producers wanted to use the stars of the show in various productions. In just a couple of years, British theatres were packed with fans desperate to catch a glimpse of their hero or heroine as they appeared in countless pantomimes every Christmas, and the top ten had a couple of new stars too.

Kylie Minogue was the first of the *Neighbours'* stars to have a stab at the recording industry, but the single that launched her singing career only came about by accident. She arrived on the doorstep of record producers Mike Stock and Matt Aitken with only an hour to spare before she had to fly back to Australia. Mike and Matt hadn't been expecting the diminutive star and asked her to wait while they wrote a song for her there and then! Kylie recorded it in one take and 'I Should Be So Lucky' topped the charts for five weeks. Not bad for an hour's work!

Jason Donovan, who, of course, played Kylie's on-screen boyfriend, soon followed suit and joined Kylie in the charts. Kylie and Jason's popularity helped to raise the profile of the show and even more people started to watch. At the same time, Kylie and Jason's greatest storyline – Scott and Charlene's wedding – was taking place on screen and their popularity spiralled into a frenzy.

In 1988, at the Australian television equivalent of the Oscars – the Logies – Kylie took the ceremony by storm, winning an unrivalled four awards in the one night. She even picked up the Gold Logie for Most Popular Television Personality. Jason picked up the award for Most Popular Actor on the same night, and *Neighbours* itself also won in the Most Popular Drama Series category, but instead of celebrating, Kylie returned to her hotel room where she collapsed in tears. The arduous workload and constant pressure of being in the hottest show on the planet had finally got to her. The attention of the press didn't help either, and all the stars of *Neighbours* found that the tiniest aspects of their personal lives had suddenly become big news. One British paper realized just how popular the show was and offered a competition to win a trip to the *Neighbours* set. The newspaper's offices and staff were swamped with a staggering one million entries – in just three days!

Kylie and Jason may have been the ultimate boy- and girl-next-door for millions of viewers right around the world, but of course it wasn't just these two who signalled the soap's success. The sunny location scenes and the lack of poverty certainly contrasted with the usual British fare of gritty, grimy soaps like *Coronation Street* and *EastEnders*. Some experts also claimed that *Neighbours'* commitment to family values had particular resonance for a society just starting to come to terms with AIDS. Whether or not that's true, the after-school timeslot certainly helped and *Neighbours* became the perfect way to relax from the day into the evening for millions of UK viewers.

Of course it's impossible to single out any one particular reason why *Neighbours* has been so spectacularly successful for a decade now, but whatever the recipe's secret ingredient is, it's certainly a magic blend.

Naturally, when anything gets as much attention as *Neighbours* has had, not all of it will be appreciative. Some claimed the plots were silly and unrealistic, others said that it set a bad example for teenagers who were rarely seen doing their homework, and even the TV watchdogs criticized it for failing to feature any racial minorities – and showing too many adults drinking alcohol!

All the criticisms were taken on board, which made *Neighbours* a stronger show that continued to find the international pulse and create storylines for the never-ending supply of engaging characters.

Birthdays are always occasions to celebrate, and *Neighbours'* tenth birthday is certainly a milestone that's no exception. It's worthy of commemoration because never before has one show entertained everyone from royalty (both Princess Diana and the Queen Mum are rumoured to be addicts of the soap) to university students to mums and kids at home. The reason for the show's success will no doubt always remain a mystery, but because it never fails to entertain you can bet that in ten years' time we'll be cracking open the champagne for another celebration and to toast *Neighbours* a happy twentieth birthday!

SPORTS OVAL

NUMBER
22

When *Neighbours* first started in 1986, number 22 was unoccupied. But it was only to be a couple of months before Max Ramsay started getting suspicious about the toings and froings at what he called 'The Ape House', so named because the only 'people' seen entering and leaving the house were dressed as gorillas. But we were soon to learn that they were in fact gibbons; Clive Gibbons, Ramsay Street's newest resident, who ran a gorilla-gram service.

Clive was quite a shock to the sleepy suburban cul-de-sac, but he was also a breath of fresh air. He was one of life's eccentrics who'd turned his back on medicine after failing to save his girlfriend's life. But he still took good care of people and offered a bed to plenty of waifs and strays in their hour of need, who he usually also lured into his latest harebrained scheme.

Clive rented the house from an absentee landlord, from whom Paul Robinson bought the deeds in 1988 when the Daniels Corporation tried to acquire the land Ramsay Street was built on for a supermarket development. When the deal fell through, Paul was still the owner of number 22 and decided to live there himself. It wasn't long before he'd moved in his friend from his airline days and new number two at Lassiters, Gail Lewis. Gail was a businesswoman whose brain was as smart as her suits, and who was so dedicated to her career that men didn't get a look in. So when one of Lassiters' Japanese clients, Mr Udugawa, was looking to place a big new contract in Australia but would rather deal with a family man, marrying Paul made perfect sense. It was a way they could both further their careers and, anyway, they had both been married and divorced

Neighbours

before (Paul to Terri Inglis and Gail to racing driver Jeremy Lord). Without any fuss, they arranged for a minister to come to the house and marry them in front of a few family members and friends before going to sleep in separate bedrooms.

Predictably, Gail soon found herself falling for her husband, but Paul – as ever – was too involved with work to notice. In the end Gail found the situation unbearable and took another job overseas. It took Paul's younger brother Scott to point out what had been glaringly obvious to viewers for months, and Paul realized that he loved Gail as much as she loved him and got to her just in time before a taxi took her to the airport and out of his life forever. But once they tore up their pre-nuptial agreement and started sharing a bed, Gail had to come clean about something it hadn't been necessary to mention when the marriage had been one of convenience: she couldn't have children.

Paul was keen to start a family and so he and Gail embarked on IVF treatment when, out of the blue, Paul discovered he was already a father. An old friend both he and Gail had known when they worked for the airline came to stay at Lassiters with her two-year-old daughter, Amy. When the friend learnt that Paul and Gail were having difficulty conceiving, she had to confess that Amy was in fact the result of a short fling she'd had with Paul. Gail feared that Paul would no longer want to try for children of their own, but he reassured her that he still wanted them to start a family and Gail soon announced the IVF treatment had worked and she was pregnant – with triplets!

But Paul's devotion to finding new ways to worship the dollar drove Gail away and in the end she decided to leave him and make a home for herself and their children away from Ramsay Street. Paul used his new-found single status to work even harder and moved into a suite at Lassiters so he could be closer to the office! It also meant he could make even more money by renting out number 22.

The woman who signed the lease was one Linda Giles, and she created a lot of confusion when different neighbours claimed to have seen her in different places at the same time wearing different outfits. The confusion was soon explained when Linda Giles was revealed to be Caroline *and* Christina Alessi, played by identical twins Gayle and Gillian Blakeney. Caroline had moved to the area confident that she would get Gail's job at Lassiters but didn't want to influence her chances either way by letting her prospective employer make an assessment of her before her interview. So when she realized Paul would also be her and Christina's landlord, she invented the name Linda Giles when signing the lease.

Paul found out about her deception but he couldn't care less: he had fallen for Linda Giles and was so taken with her he forgave the twins. The only problem now was that he didn't know which of them he fancied! But, as he had learnt about mixing business with pleasure before, the safer recipient for his affection was Chrissie, who had none of her sister's ambition to make it big in business. In almost every other way, however, the sisters were identical. And they were also exceptionally close; woe betide the man who came between these two sisters.

Although Caroline was happy for her sister and her boss – even when Paul moved in with them – there was always a little twinge of regret that Chrissie had got to him first. Both twins had confessed that they fancied their new landlord when they arrived in Ramsay Street, and so the wheels were set in motion for one of *Neighbours'* best ever love triangles. As Chrissie planned her wedding to Paul and had a baby, Andrew, with him, Caroline kept her mouth shut. But when the pressure started to mount at work, it was Caroline Paul felt he could confide in. She knew the pressures he was under, whereas his wife only understood that he wasn't spending enough time with her and their son. One night, when Chrissie had banished Paul to the sofa, Caroline came home to find her brother-in-law asleep and went to cover him with a blanket. In doing so she accidentally woke him and the two shared a passionate embrace. This was made more enticing for the viewers because of the well-publicized off-screen romance between Gayle Blakeney and Stefan Dennis, who played Paul. Paul couldn't pretend that he'd confused

CHRISTINA ALESSI

Gayle Blakeney

Chrissie moved to the street in March 1991 to be with her twin sister, Caroline, who had landed a job at Lassiters. Unlike her twin, Chrissie's ambition in life was to be a good wife and mother. She was instantly attracted to local tycoon Paul Robinson and they married in February 1992. Chrissie surprised her sister and her husband by running the Lassiters gift shop with flair and at a profit, but when she became pregnant she was more than happy to give up work to be a full-time mum, and when Paul had his breakdown she was as supportive as she could be. But when she discovered her sister and her husband had been having an affair it was her who needed the sympathy. However, Paul and Chrissie reunited and left Ramsay Street with their son, Andrew, for a new life in Hawaii. They now live in Rio where Paul is avoiding arrest for fraud.

Caroline for Christina – he knew full well which sister he'd kissed – and it was the exciting climax of a storyline that had been built up over years.

Caroline was so ashamed of having kissed her sister's husband that she packed her bags and left for a new job in Milan within days. She said a tearful goodbye to her twin who didn't really understand her sister's sudden departure but, sure enough, over the next few weeks the penny dropped with a resounding thud and Chrissie confronted Paul with her suspicions. He couldn't deny it and so, distraught, Chrissie threw him out and told him he would never see his son again.

After much huffing and puffing and demanding access to Andrew, Paul's granny Helen eventually made him realize that the only way he was going to get his wife and son back was to make Chrissie see that he was truly sorry – and truly committed to their future. He undertook to be a better person, was conciliatory and respectful. It was a side of Paul the neighbours had never seen before, and he assured them it wasn't an act: Chrissie and Andrew were the most important people in his world and he would do whatever it took. And sure enough, in time, Chrissie came round and the two renewed their vows at a special ceremony before leaving for a new life in Hawaii.

Number 22 was then occupied by the twins' cousin Marco who was soon joined by his younger brother, Rick, who had run away from a posh boarding school. Marco was one of life's drifters, floating from one dead-end job to another, so his parents, Benito and Cathy, had invested their hopes for the future in son number two. But Rick's attitude to work was even more slack than his brother's: always put off till tomorrow what's too much effort to do today. Cathy and Benito were quick to arrive in Erinsborough so they could force Rick to go back to his school. But there was no way Rick was going back – even if he had wanted to, the school wouldn't have him because he'd been expelled. So Cathy and Benito decided to stay put in Ramsay Street and sort their sons out.

Paul offered his wife's uncle the top job at Lassiters, while Cathy bought the lease of the Coffee Shop where she wowed her customers with her secret spaghetti sauce. Meanwhile, their sons tried to find love – Marco without success but Rick fell head over heels for Debbie Martin. It was an intense relationship for two teenagers and both the Alessis and the Martins kept a careful eye on the lovebirds, making sure they didn't get up to no good. But Cathy was soon to become preoccupied with having another baby. Hanging around pregnant Phoebe Bright had made her broody and she told her husband she wanted to be a mum again. Benito told her this was impossible, for the simple reason that he'd had a vasectomy several years before. Cathy was upset but forced to admit that her broodiness was tied up with guilt at having given up their first child for adoption when they were sixteen. Cathy and Benito had been childhood sweethearts, but when their families discovered Cathy was going to be a gymslip mum, they persuaded the young couple to give their daughter, Lindsay, up for adoption.

The news that he wasn't their eldest child affected Marco deeply, and against his parents' wishes he tracked down his long-lost sister. It was a tense reunion for the Alessis and, ultimately, an unfulfilling one, as Lindsay declared that she would rather get on with her own life, although she did agree to stay in touch with her natural family.

Marco's Italian hot headedness often got him into trouble, especially where money was concerned. If he saw a nice designer jacket he would have to have it, even if he couldn't afford it. Not surprisingly, it was only a matter of time before he found himself in debt. But he couldn't borrow money from his disciplinarian father for fear of a lecture on money management, so he turned to a loan shark and pretty soon he was up to his neck not just in debt, but in trouble. The loan shark's heavies were on his back daily, so when the opportunity came to chaperone Rick and Debbie on a trip to London, Marco leapt at the chance. But wherever Marco went, the loan shark had contacts and even in London he couldn't get away from his debts. One day, when Debbie and Rick

were off sightseeing, Marco slipped away, never to be seen again – although he did send his parents a postcard from Italy to say he was all right.

Rick returned to Erinsborough to face his parents' fury. Cathy and Benito had strictly forbidden him to see Debbie, and to learn that the teenagers had not only been together but also sneaked away to the other side of the world was unforgiveable behaviour. The two were grounded while Helen, who had also accompanied the teenagers, explained that Rick had won a competition to see Michael Jackson in London and that they had felt it had been too good an opportunity to miss.

Cathy and Benito eventually mellowed, but when Ben was offered a new job in Sydney they saw it as the perfect way to take Rick away from Debbie and make him knuckle down for his HSC. Debbie was horrified that Rick might soon be leaving and so the two decided to show their love for each other and sleep

together. Rick was so thrilled at this development in their relationship that he resolved to stay in Erinsborough and arranged for an AusStudy grant and a room at Lassiters in exchange for working in the kitchens. His parents couldn't refuse; Rick had shown them that he was committed to Debbie and responsible enough to support himself, and they had to admit that that was all they'd ever really wanted from their son. They therefore allowed him to stay in Erinsborough when they moved to Sydney.

Number 22 was empty for a while but news soon filtered back to Ramsay Street that Paul had rented out the house, and the neighbours anticipated the arrival of new residents. Some were in for a shock when the Lim family moved in. This Chinese immigrant family stood out in the lily-white suburb and some of the neighbours, notably Julie Martin, had a hard time concealing their racism. The Lims had come to Erinsborough while Raymond Lim undertook some work in the neighbourhood, but his six-week contract came to an end and speculation again mounted as to who would move into the street.

The new owner was brash and brazen Lotto winner Cheryl Stark, who had been pursuing Lou Carpenter without success for a couple of months. Cheryl, who had gone to the bother of contacting Paul in Hawaii about the deeds, was shortly joined at number 22 by her younger children, Brett and Danni (she has two other children, trouble-maker Darren and Janine who's in the Navy), who wanted to leave the boarding schools they were attending and live with their mother. At first Cheryl didn't want them with her because she was enjoying the independence her Lotto

BRETT STARK
Brett Blewitt

Brett is the sort of boy most girls call a nerd. He's not particularly good-looking, is bookish, knows lots of useless information about the lifecycle of fruit flies and gets tongue-twisted in the presence of girls. But Brett is also one of the kindest people who has ever lived in Ramsay Street, and while his hot-headed sister Danni disapproved of their mum's relationship with Lou, Brett was always supportive. He was the first to congratulate them when Cheryl became pregnant. Brett has had a few encounters with girls but it wasn't until his mum's golfing buddy, Judy Bergman, saw the man inside the boy that he started his first passionate affair in 1996. When it ended, Brett was forced to leave Ramsay Street for good.

win had given her and she knew they wouldn't approve of her flaunting herself in front of Lou. But Brett and Danni knew they could make their mum feel guilty about neglecting her maternal duties, and it didn't take long before the two teenagers were enrolled at Erinsborough High and getting into trouble with the local kids.

Danni had an instant attraction with bad boy Michael Martin and the two would sneak off whenever they could, jumping

DANNI STARK
Eliza Szonert

Danni moved into Ramsay Street and immediately got the neighbours talking when Michael Martin caught her injecting herself with a needle. Everyone had to admit that she was pretty moody, and soon everyone became convinced she was using drugs. Danni even played along with the image, as she was glad of the attention after years of emotional neglect at boarding school. But Danni was a diabetic, not a heroin addict, and when Michael found out that she had been stringing him along he blew up at her. Danni, however, was already smitten with him and made a play for his affections. The two had a passionate relationship – even making love without using contraception once – but in time it fizzled out. Danni later took up with Mal Kennedy and the two moved into a room together at number 32.

out of bedroom windows and shimmying down trees to snatch an illicit evening together. One night they went to a club, and when Danni, a diabetic, started feeling faint she went outside and collapsed. The police picked her up assuming she was just another underage drinker who couldn't handle her grog, and put her in the cells to dry out. But she hadn't been drinking, she'd just forgotten to take her insulin and slipped into a coma. Michael panicked when he couldn't find her and he was forced to call his and Danni's folks to enlist their help in finding Danni before it was too late. Michael eventually stumbled into the right police station and got Danni to a hospital just in time. No matter how cross the parents were that they'd been disobeyed, they were so relieved at Michael's quick thinking and devotion that he was hailed as a hero, and the two were allowed to carry on seeing each other.

Brett, on the other hand, was having no luck in love and at one point had to confess to Rick Alessi that he was still a virgin. Rick, currently going through a 'treat 'em mean and keep 'em keen' phase, undertook to teach the innocent Brett about the ways of women. But Brett saw how Rick was hurting the girls he was dumping on, and resolved to wait for the right girl. In the meantime he was much happier studying or spending time with Mrs Daniels, with whom he formed a close relationship.

Brett might not have been blessed with great looks or a teriffic body, but he had a sense of humour and a sense of dignity that, one day, one woman would find irresistable – although he mostly brought out girls' maternal sides.

Cheryl finally succeeded in sinking her highly polished nails into Lou, but once

LOU CARPENTER

Tom Oliver

Lou had fancied Madge Ramsay ever since they were at school together, and when he heard she was about to marry Harold Bishop he came to Ramsay Street to try and stop her. He'd become a millionaire selling cars, but by the time he returned to Erinsborough after Harold's death in 1992 he'd lost his fortune. He still wanted to marry Madge, however, even though he had been married twice before and had three children. Madge soon left for a new life in Brisbane, but Lou stayed on and opened a car yard, Carpenter's Cars. Lou, a loveable, good-hearted and sociable man, was soon to be hounded by the irrepressible Cheryl Stark who had decided she wanted him, and what Cheryl wants, she gets. They have a daughter, Louise, and she's proof – if any were needed – of their commitment to each other. Lou's favourite place in Erinsborough is easily The Waterhole where he's spent many hours with drinking buddies Jim, Doug and Philip, and at one point Lou even sold his home brew, 'Lou's Lager', at the bar before Cheryl made his dreams come true by buying the joint: his favourite person was now running his favourite place!

they had decided to live together there was just one small problem – which house would they live in? Naturally, Danni was keen for Cheryl and Lou to have the privacy of number 24 to themselves while Danni, Brett and Lauren (Lou's daughter) and Rick, who were lodging at Lou's, shared number 22. But the thought of all those teenage hormones running wild without supervision filled the adults with horror, and Cheryl and Lou decided the whole family would live at number 24. Naturally, things were a little crowded, but once Lauren left for Hong Kong and Rick moved into number 30, the Carpenter/Stark family settled in up the road. When Cheryl discovered she was pregnant and Madge asked Lou if he would sell number 24 on her behalf, Cheryl and Lou moved their brood back to number 22, where they were joined in 1995 by baby Louise. Lou and Cheryl's commitment to each other was about to be put to two very demanding tests. The first came when Lou's daughter from a teenage fling came to Erinsborough to look him up. Lou had kept Mai Ling Chan – he had had a holiday romance with her mother over thirty years before – a secret from Cheryl because he just hadn't found the right time to tell her. But if that wasn't a big enough test, when Lou's second wife, Linda, turned up in Ramsay Street, she put Cheryl and Lou's relationship in a tight spot. Linda told them that if she re-married Lou, an old relative's will stipulated she would inherit a lot of money. And so Lou had to decide between Cheryl or the money.

NUMBER 24

No matter who lives at number 24, it will always be referred to as 'The Ramsay House', even though the last Ramsay left it behind in 1993 when Madge moved to Brisbane. But until then, a Ramsay had lived on the street since it was built. The house got its name from Max Ramsay's granddad, Jack, and Max was always proprietorial about what he saw as 'his' street where he lived with his European wife, Maria, and their sons, Shane and Danny.

Max was a real larrakin and those who employed him as a plumber often found him taking a beer break. He was the sort of man who would tell his sons, 'Do what I say, not what I do'. He wanted nothing but the best for his boys, so when Shane showed potential as a diver, Max trained him himself and pushed him as hard as he could until a car smash injured Shane's back and put paid to those dreams of Olympic gold – and those poolside scenes in swimming trunks! Max came across as a bully, but whereas Shane could take his foghorn father's outbursts, the gentler Danny couldn't. Max thought Danny was a wimp and wished he'd be more like Shane who was as good with the girls as he was with the boys down the pub.

The Ramsays were a good foil to the better bred Robinsons, but they were always neighbourly to each other. Shane and Paul were best mates and Helen and Maria often confided in each other. But the suburban status quo was about to be shattered when Maria revealed that Danny was not Max's son. Max's pride was fatally wounded and he moved out into a bedsit, taking Shane's loyalty with him. It split the family in two, and when Maria started seeing another man, Shane and Danny had to face the fact their parents'

marriage was over. Maria and Danny moved to Brisbane and Max's sister Madge moved in to make sure Max and Shane were taken care of. Madge and Shane raised the money to buy number 24, so when Max got back together with Maria and joined her in Brisbane, Madge stayed on in the house.

Before long, Madge's daughter Charlene (played memorably by the then unknown Kylie Minogue) moved in and they prepared for her son Henry's release from prison. Madge's children, by ex-husband Fred Mitchell, were going to be trouble. It was revealed that Charlene had had an abortion, been on the pill and generally caused her mother so much grief that she'd been sent to live with her father. Henry, on the other hand, had simply fallen in with the wrong crowd. Nevertheless, his criminal record meant the local residents were wary of him, and when he took over his cousin Shane's gardening business, some thought it would allow him to gain access to their houses.

But Ramsay Street was to be the making of them. Henry's business took off and Charlene fell hook, line and sinker for the boy next door, Scott Robinson, played by Kylie Minogue's rumoured boyfriend Jason Donovan. Theirs was a teen romance to rival Romeo and Juliet's and the Ramsays and the Robinsons did pretty good impressions of the Montagues and the Capulets as they tried to keep the two of them apart. It's a frequent storyline in *Neighbours* where teen love is disapproved of so that whenever the lovers steal a moment together it is seen as a triumph by the millions of teenagers who watch around the world. But no teen romance before or since has captured the imaginations of the viewers like Scott and Charlene's. And when Jim and Madge refused to let them live together, the impetuous Scott skateboarded over to the garage where Charlene was working as an apprentice to ask her to marry him. She accepted, and the biggest – and most romantic – wedding Ramsay Street had ever seen was planned.

On 8 November 1988 Henry gave his little sister away to the happiest groom in the world in a perfect fairytale service. They exchanged vows and after a short reception at the Robinsons', the young couple honeymooned in Surfer's Paradise. When they returned they shared Charlene's old room at number 24 where Scott studied hard to get a cadetship as a journalist on the local paper and Charlene carried on her mechanic's apprenticeship at Rob Lewis's garage.

Number 24 was soon to have another occupant, one of Madge's childhood sweethearts, Harold Bishop. When Shane and Charlene learnt that Harold was visiting Erinsborough on business in June 1988, they arranged for him to meet Madge. And when the two came face to face after so many years, it was clear there was still something between them, even though they were as different as chalk and cheese. Madge was bolshy and emotional, Harold was reserved and timid, but the genuine affection between them shone through and theirs was, in fact, one of the strongest relationships in Ramsay Street. When Harold was weak, Madge would bully him. When Madge opened her mouth before thinking and hurt other people's feelings, Harold would pacify. Throughout their engagement Harold lodged at Mrs Mangel's because it would have been improper for them to live together before they were married, but after their wedding in the summer of 1989 Harold made number 24 his home.

It was time for Shane to move on and he took off on his motorbike to see Australia (even though his swimming trophies were still to be seen on the sideboard for a couple of years!), but there was always enough drama at number 24 for him not to be missed. For starters there was another romance, and this time it was Henry's turn for love. After a series of disastrous girlfriends (including Melanie Pearson who was to return as a major character a couple of years later), he fell for neighbour Bronwyn Davies who lived at number 28 and was Jamie Clark's nanny.

Henry's sister's marriage went through a rocky patch when Charlene started taking driving lessons and Scott thought her instructor was paying his wife more attention than was necessary. However, the real

threat to their union came when Charlene's best friend and bridesmaid, 'plain' Jane 'superbrain' Harris, started tutoring Scott when he was resitting his HSC. She was the first person who read his work, and therefore she was the first person who ever praised him as a writer, which meant a lot to Scott. As his exams drew closer, and the more time he spent studying with Jane, it was clear they were falling for each other. But as he was married to her best friend, there was no way Jane was going to act on her emotions.

One day, while they were studying out at Lassiters' lake, Scott was overcome and leaned over and kissed Jane – just at the moment his brother-in-law Henry walked past to do some gardening. Henry confronted Jane with what he had seen and she didn't deny it, after all it had meant nothing to her and hadn't led anywhere. But Henry felt he had to tell his kid sister, who fumed like a chimney when she heard what had happened. Scott was thrown out and moved back to his dad's at number 26 with his tail between his legs, all the while wondering how a little kiss could lead to the break-up of his marriage. Jane, meanwhile, went to America on business for the new Robinson Corporation and when she returned several weeks later she was amazed to learn that Charlene still hadn't forgiven Scott. So she marched over to number 24 and told Charlene that if she didn't want Scott, then she would have him – or any number of other girls would, for that matter. It was enough to make Charlene realize what she had in Scott and she went round to number 26 for a reunion.

Charlene's grandparents, Dan and Edna, were so impressed by the young couple's commitment to each other that they bought them a house as a belated wedding present. Scott and Charlene were delighted, until they found out that the house was in Brisbane. The talked it over and decided it was too good an offer to refuse – after all, they'd never lived on their own – and Charlene packed her bags while Scott stayed on until he could transfer his cadetship to a newspaper in Queensland. After a couple of months he followed his wife and, for short time, things seemed pretty quiet at number 24. But not for long …

Madge's experience with Scott and Charlene proved to her that young people are ready for more serious relationships than she had given them credit for, so when Henry and Bronwyn got engaged, Bronwyn was welcomed into the house with open arms. But then Bronwyn was the sort of girl every mum wants her son to marry; she was smart, capable and caring. Not only had she looked after Des's son Jamie, she had also taken care of her younger sister, Sharon, who was a handful to say the least. But childcare was not her chosen vocation, what she really wanted to be was a vet. And Henry needed someone with ambition, because he was the sort of person who was happy if the sun was shining and the pubs were open at the same time. Henry was good working for himself, largely because he didn't have the discipline to work for anybody else and was too zany to apply himself to any one task for very long. And anyway, he could get a good tan working in gardens all day long.

But Henry's larger-than-life personality brought him to the attentions of a talent scout who found a job for him – as a DJ at a radio station in New Zealand. This was a big move for the former prison inmate and a chance he never thought he'd have, so he and Bronwyn said a very tearful farewell to each other at the airport before Henry flew off to start a new life. Bronwyn stayed behind, and Madge, who had grown very fond of her, was glad to have Bronwyn stay until she could find veterinary work in New Zealand. When Bronnie did leave a couple of months later it was to marry Henry, but the house wasn't empty for long …

Madge's niece Gemma came to stay, as did Harold's son David and his daughter Kerry, and her daughter Sky. Gemma was Max and Madge's younger brother Tom's daughter, and she came to stay with her aunt so she could knuckle down for her HSC. Once her schooling was done, this sensitive country girl started working in the Coffee Shop before she found a job in an animal sanctuary. Her work clothes were the overalls that had been handed down from Shane and Henry from the gardening days, to Charlene for her mechanic's work and to Bronwyn for when she worked with animals. But Gemma's

MADGE BISHOP

Anne Charleston

When Madge first arrived in Ramsay Street in 1987 many of the neighbours found her a bit uppity. She came across as if she thought she was better than her larrakin brothers, Max and Tom, but in truth she was just worried about what the neighbours might think of her! Madge was born in Brisbane where she dated Lou Carpenter and Harold Bishop as a teenager, but she dashed both their hopes when she married local bad boy Fred Mitchell, with whom she had two children, Henry and Charlene. Despite fighting with their mum, these two actually thought the world of her. After an acrimonious divorce from Fred, she married Harold but was widowed after only three years. Despite advances from Lou, she returned to Brisbane where she takes care of her grandson Daniel.

biggest reason for staying around in Erinsborough after her exams was her new boyfriend, Matt Williams.

David, Harold's son, was a carbon copy of his stuffed shirt of a father, and who came to visit a couple of times out of duty and to get to know his new step-mum. But Kerry was cut from different cloth and had railed against her father's conservatism. She'd backpacked round the world, lived in communes and – most shockingly to her father – had a child out of wedlock. Travelling round the world with a baby in her backpack was harder than hippie Kerry had imagined, and so she came to live with her dad at 24 Ramsay Street, bringing her daughter, Sky, with her.

Harold didn't really understand his daughter – the only thing they saw eye to eye on was vegetarianism, something

Neighbours

HAROLD BISHOP
Ian Smith

Harold was everything Madge wasn't: indecisive, considerate, stuffy and reserved. Some people would have no problem calling him boring. After his first wife, with whom he had two children, Kerry and David, died, he came to Erinsborough on business. Charlene seized the opportunity to do a little match-making on her mum's behalf and got the two old flames together. Harold was a practising Christian who would never miss church on a Sunday, and was an enthusiastic Scout leader. He was a bit of prude and wouldn't live with Madge until they were married – when a mix-up meant they had to share a hotel bedroom he insisted on building a wall of pillows between them! Harold had previously owned a health food store and when he took over the Coffee Shop he temporarily introduced an unpopular vegetarian menu. Harold died in 1992 when he was washed off rocks into the sea, although his body was never found.

Harold had adopted for health reasons but Kerry had turned to on principle. She brought a breath of fresh air into Ramsay Street with her campaigns to free school mice from the science labs and encouraging everyone to leave their cars behind and walk everywhere. What was really surprising though was that she fell for local oik Joe Mangel. Kerry might not have known which fork to use at formal functions but at least she knew not to use her fingers; Joe, on the other hand, had even fewer social graces than he did qualifications. But Kerry recognized that he had a heart of gold and was totally devoted to her. They were both single parents and it made sense for the two of them to live together, and so Kerry and Sky moved across the road.

Madge and Harold didn't have any trouble filling their time, because if Sky and her new step-brother Toby weren't round visiting their gran and granddad, Harold was leading the local Scout troop or Madge was running for election to the local council. But when Kerry was killed in October 1991, Harold was inconsolable.

Madge tried everything she could to lift her husband out of depression, but his daughter's death saddened Harold to his core. In the end, Madge thought a spell away from Ramsay Street and reminders of Kerry would be good for him, and as they had recently come up trumps on the premium bonds, they decided to buy a caravan and tour the country.

While they were away they rented the house to Brenda Riley, who revealed herself to be the younger sister of Harold's rival for Madge's affections when they'd been at school, Lou Carpenter. Madge made Brenda promise that she wouldn't tell Harold who she was for fear Harold would 'have a heart attack' just on hearing Lou's name again after all these years. Once Madge and Harold had left for their trip, Lou's son Guy moved in with Brenda and his good looks and way with the cappuccino machine in the Coffee Shop set his female customers' hearts aflutter. Madge and Harold felt they'd left the house and the Coffee Shop – which they owned at the time – in safe hands. But the holiday that was supposed to be a tonic for them turned out to be a disaster. When they were only a few days into their trip, Harold took a walk along some cliffs while Madge talked to a local artist. When she turned round Harold was nowhere to be seen and it was assumed he'd fallen into the sea below after Madge found his glasses in a rock pool, but his body was never found.

Distraught, Madge returned to Ramsay Street to be with her friends. Brenda offered to move out but Madge assured her she was glad of the company and for several months Madge, Brenda and Guy lived together relatively peacefully. But it was the calm before the storm: Lou was about to return and Lou was as loud and brash as they come.

Lou was a bit of a flash harry, having been a millionaire (a fortune he accrued in the second-hand car business), he was used to getting his own way and he didn't mind paying for it. He'd now lost his fortune, but he still liked to get his own way. Beneath his medallion-man image, however, Lou was a loving, funny man who was painfully aware that time was not on his side. Although Brenda was pleased to see her brother, Guy and Madge were not. Guy had resented his father since his parents' marriage broke up and the two men hadn't spoken in years. Madge didn't want him around because it was clear Lou still fancied his luck with her, and as she was still mourning Harold she wanted to avoid any unwelcome advances.

As Madge watched Lou repair his relationship with his son, she saw a softer side to him and she realized, as did Guy before he left, that he'd grown up and sorted out his priorities. He might always try to turn every situation into a joke, but after so much sadness it was refreshing to be around someone who always tried to find the funny side. And so, for a while, Madge and Lou rekindled the romance they'd had when they were at school together in Queensland. Lou was smitten and proposed, but his offer of marriage made Madge discover that she was a long way off being over Harold and she turned him down, announcing that she was going to live with Scott and Charlene in Brisbane.

As Lou had started a new business in Erinsborough, Carpenter's Cars, and his devoted daughter Lauren had come to live with him, he decided to stay put and rent the house from Madge. But her rejection of him hit him badly, and as he turned fifty he began to think his best years were behind him. So when his lodger, Beth Brennan, brought her friend, Annalise Hartman – a drop-dead gorgeous, blonde model of a girl – round to see if she would like to rent the spare room, Lou's tongue hung out like a dog's. And when Annalise seemed to be interested in him, his heart skipped a thousand beats.

It was a classic example of the male menopause and Lou made himself look ridiculous as he tried to keep up with his much younger girlfriend. He tried break dancing and took to wearing a baseball cap the wrong way round and, frankly, looked quite pathetic. But he was so besotted with the blonde lovely in hot pants that he proposed – and Annalise accepted. Annalise's mother, Fiona, had something to say about the impending nuptials; didn't Lou know she was only seventeen? He didn't. He'd thought she was at least twenty-one, and told Annalise he couldn't marry someone younger than his own daughter. However, he allowed her to continue to rent a room from him.

The house was heaving with teenagers: as well as Annalise, Beth and Lauren, Rick Alessi also moved in after his mum visited from Sydney and asked Lou to keep an eye on him. Having so many young people around was enough to rejuvenate Lou, and he started acting his age again.

And Lauren was about to need all her father's years of wisdom since she had got herself in hot – if not boiling – water: she had started an affair with her best friend Beth's fiancé, Brad Willis.

Lauren and Brad first saw each other when he was down at the beach catching the early morning surf and she was riding her horse. Their eyes met and there was an instant attraction. They stopped and talked for a while but then left without exchanging names.

So when Lauren rode her horse into Ramsay Street a week or so later, Brad got the surprise of his life. Despite the fact that he was already engaged to Beth, Brad couldn't deny the chemistry that existed between him and Lauren and the two conducted an affair in secret. Lauren didn't even tell her dad, as Lou had become so fond of Beth since she'd been lodging with him. But when Lauren thought she was pregnant, she couldn't hide it from her dad any longer. Lou was shocked, but stood by his little girl when he found a pregnancy test kit in her cupboard. It turned out she wasn't pregnant, but she did have a venereal disease which Brad feared he could pass on to Beth. Despite pleas from Lou, Brad and Lauren just couldn't help themselves, but Brad could not extricate himself from the wedding plans which were being made apace. And Beth was so blinded with love for Brad that she had no idea anything was wrong until it was too late.

It wasn't until she was walking down the aisle and saw how her groom looked at Lauren, who was her bridesmaid, that the pieces fell into place. When she was asked if she would 'take this man', she had to reply that she didn't, and left the ceremony in tears.

Beth went away after the wedding, leaving Brad and Lauren to see each other openly. But it soon became clear that the chemistry between them was just an inconclusive experiment and the two went their own separate ways. Lauren was now in desperate need of some friends and found herself drawn into a religious cult. Lou was worried about his daughter but a rather large distraction in the shape of Cheryl Stark was vying for his attention. Cheryl first came to Ramsay Street when her wayward son Darren got mixed up with the Martin kids after he'd been in a detention centre with Michael. And as soon as she clapped eyes on Lou she decided she was going to have him.

Cheryl used to run a pub, but since winning the Lotto jackpot, she had sold the pub and was amusing herself spending her fortune. In one day she bought four cars from Lou's car yard just so she could talk to him. Lou had never met a woman with as much front as Cheryl Stark and tried to run away from her man-eating ways. Eventually the message seemed to sink in and Cheryl went as quickly as she'd come.

This allowed Lou time to rescue Lauren from the cult which had started to brainwash her. Lauren's friends were turning against her and Lou feared he might lose her for good. But when Lauren was asked by the leader of the cult to sleep with him, she came to her senses and left.

While Lou was relieved to see Lauren out of the cult's clutches, he was panicked by the re-emergence of Cheryl Stark who, it turned out, had bought number 22 from Paul Robinson. She was back, and this time she wasn't going to take no for an answer. Cheryl decided to play it cool with Lou this time because she knew the hard sell didn't work, and in time her plan paid off. And that left them with the problem of which house to live in?

In the end they compromised. Because Cheryl refused to marry Lou, as he would have liked, she pacified him by agreeing to move her brood into his house. Things were going to be a little crowded. Although Annalise had since moved in with Helen Daniels at number 26, Rick was forced to share a room with Brett, and Lauren had to share with Danni. But not for long, as Lauren landed a job as a jockey's groom in Hong Kong. Lou was naturally broken-hearted to see his little girl go off to another country, but as it had always been her dream to work with horses he knew she would be happy.

Just as the Stark/Carpenter brood were getting settled, Madge pulled the rug from under them when she wrote to Lou and asked him to sell up. At least they still had number 22 to move in to. The house was sold to a mysterious woman who hadn't bothered to inspect the place before she bought it, and this aroused great suspicion about the new neighbour. Before she arrived, she sent her grandson, Sam Kratz, to check the joint out.

Sam, a handsome biker always on the edge of the law, hit it off with Brett and Danni who looked up to him and thought he was glamorous. And when Sam's gran, Marlene, arrived on the scene she said she was glad he'd got to know the two Stark children because they were in fact his cousins: Marlene was Cheryl's estranged mother.

The two women hadn't seen each other since Cheryl was a little girl and it was clear Cheryl resented her mother. Marlene wasn't expecting a big welcome, so she told Sam to keep her secret until the time was right. Like all secrets in Ramsay Street, it wasn't long before Cheryl found out that Marlene was her mother and she felt compromised that Marlene had

SAM KRATZ
Richard Grieve

When Madge Ramsay asked Lou Carpenter to sell number 24 for her, he thought he had sold to an older woman. So when leather-clad twentysomething Sam roared into the street, he was immediately suspicious. And when it seemed Sam had sold Lou's things, which were still in storage at the house, Lou was ready to call the police. But Sam explained that he thought the stuff belonged to his gran, the woman who owned the house now. After a shaky start, and recovering Lou's things, Sam became very popular in Ramsay Street – especially with Annalise Hartman who he started dating after she'd been jilted at the altar by Mark Gottlieb. Sam may look rough, with his stubble and oil stains, but he has proven himself to be a rough diamond.

bought a house so close to her own. But as Brett and Danni made friends with the gran they'd never known, Cheryl got to know Marlene better and eventually had to admit that she quite liked the old girl – although she never could bring herself to call her 'mum'.

Marlene busied herself with various scams including selling make-up to the neighbours, but she found herself a nice little earner when she opened up a 'trash and treasure' store (and the rent she got from Cody Willis who moved into one of the spare rooms), and like most people she even found love in the unlikely form of new coffee-shop manager Colin Taylor, a fact fan and trivia head of annoying proportions.

It was never going to be long before one of the women in Ramsay Street got her

MARLENE KRATZ
Moya O'Sullivan

Marlene bought number 24 without even seeing it because she had heard her estranged daughter, Cheryl, was living in the street and after a quarter of a century apart, Marlene thought it was time to build some bridges. Marlene had left when Cheryl was eleven and in the intervening years, Cheryl had demonized her mother in her mind so when she found out who Marlene was, she wanted absolutely nothing to do with her. But her grandkids, Danni and Brett, did, and gradually Cheryl came to understand her mother. And if she could one day find it in her heart to call Marlene 'mum', well nothing would make the old girl happier. Marlene is a bit scatty and is always on for a scam or a silly bet. After selling cosmetics door to door and having a neat line in second-hand VCRs, she now runs a 'trash and treasure' store in town and typically invents a story for almost every item that passes through her wacky shop.

teeth into the handsome Sam, and the woman who got to him the most was Annalise Hartman, to whom he confessed his feelings after she'd been jilted at the altar. Annalise soon moved back into her former home and, in January 1996, when Joanna, the sister she never knew she had, turned up, she was welcomed into the house too – even if she was pretty enough to make Annalise jealous. Jo was Annalise's half sister and she introduced Annalise to her father for the first time. Jo told Annalise that their father, Tarquin, was in the performing arts but Annalise didn't have a clue what to expect when she finally met him. She certainly didn't expect to meet a man wearing high heels, a blond wig and the same dress as she had on! Yes, Tarquin was actually a female impersonator who went by the name of Sequin! Still, at least they had their wardrobe in common.

Cody and Jo, on the other hand, had less than zero in common. Cody was a brainbox medical student, while Jo was even more vacuous than her blond looks would have you stereotype her. She was dizzy, forgetful and about as bright as a glowworm. And Jo's simpleness infuriated Cody so much that she moved out in April 1996 to share at number 30, leaving Annalise, Sam, Jo and Marlene at number 24.

N U M B E R
26

In 1986, when the show started, number 26 was full to capacity. Widower Jim Robinson and his kindly mother-in-law, Helen Daniels, tended to the needs of Jim's four children: Paul, an engineering undergraduate; Julie, a bank clerk; Scott, a lustful teenager; and nine-year-old Lucy. Of course, this being Ramsay Street, it wasn't long before their happy home had a few changes.

Helen had come to live with the Robinsons after her daughter Anne had died giving birth to Lucy. As Helen's husband Bill had recently died she was more than happy to come and look after her grandchildren. And boy, was she needed! The first bombshell that shook the emotional foundations of number 26 came when Paul announced he was jacking in university. Jim had always hoped Paul would one day take over the reins of his engineering firm and was horrified that his eldest son wanted to give up his degree to become an airline steward, of all things. But Paul was adamant and none of Jim and Helen's words of counsel did any good.

But then Paul was proving himself to be a very impulsive young man. When Terri Inglis started working as Max Ramsay's plumber's mate, every man in the street wanted to date her. But it was Paul, after just one date, who proposed marriage and he was over the moon when she accepted.

As a wedding present, Jim rented number 30 for the young couple, but when their marriage ended in disaster, Paul turned into a hard-hearted and selfish man who was never going to let his emotions get the better of him again. It was these qualities that led his aunt, Rosemary (Helen's adopted daughter), to offer Paul the job of running the Australian arm of her company, The Daniels Corporation, with its headquarters in the local Lassiters hotel complex.

It wasn't long before Julie moved out too, but even Helen and Jim were glad to see the back of Julie's interfering and sticky-beaking, even if they wouldn't admit it. Julie, to be honest, was a pain in the backside. If there was a wrong thing to say, she'd say it. If there was a feeling to be hurt, she'd hurt it. She also had skin thicker than an elephant's and was completely unaware that she was upsetting people. She had once dated neighbour and assistant bank manager Des Clarke, but when a new boss took over the local branch of the Pacific Bank, Julie fell for him in a big way. What she didn't know was that Philip Martin, the new manager, was married.

But even when he came clean about his wife and two children, Julie would not be put off, especially when she learnt that his wife was an alcoholic and making his life hell. The real test in their relationship came when Philip's wife, Loretta, crashed the car while drunk, killing herself and seriously injuring Philip. There was no question in Julie's mind that she wouldn't take care of her lover and his children, and she moved away from Erinsborough to be with them. Helen and Jim were chuffed to realize that Julie had a compassionate side to her, they just wished she hadn't kept it a secret from them for so many years!

Love and romance were not just the province of the young; Jim and Helen both had people come into their lives who made their hearts dance. Jim embarked on an intense romance with Daphne's friend Zoe Davis, and also with Englishwoman Ruth Williams who he met on a plane. But it wasn't until his witch-like cousin Hilary introduced him to a doctor friend of hers, Beverly Marshall, that Jim thought of marrying again.

Jim and Beverly were well matched. They both liked golf, both enjoyed the outdoors and were both professional, educated people. They would have been perfect for each other if it hadn't been for one thing: Beverly wanted children and Jim didn't. When they got married in 1989, Beverly was so busy running the local GP's practice and doing research for the local university, she didn't have time to listen to her biological clock. But when the alarm bell went off, Beverly became a hormonal mess desperate to have a child. Jim censured that they already had her niece and nephew, Katie and Todd Landers, to look after and surely they were enough of a handful. Beverly, though, was insistent and Jim agreed to start trying for another child.

Beverly became pregnant only to lose the baby during her pregnancy and the baby, a girl, was stillborn. So Beverley investigated the option of adoption – only to be turned down because Jim was too old. She was, however, able to foster and was given the charge of a baby called Rhys. But when Rhys was taken away from her it was the final staw and Beverley fell to pieces – as did her marriage.

Jim and Beverly had been driven apart by her quest for motherhood, and sad as he was to see his marriage end, Jim knew it was for the best. Beverly wanted Todd to return to her native Adelaide (Katie had returned a year or so before), but Todd was in love with Cody Willis and at a critical point in his school career, so Jim agreed that he could stay.

JIM ROBINSON

Alan Dale

Jim Robinson is the sort of man other men tend to hate. He had it all; his own business, a big house, lovely kids, a way with women. But it all went wrong when his wife Anne died giving birth to their youngest child, Lucy. After Anne's death there was always a reserved sadness about him, and at times he came across as stuffy and proper, but there was never anything he wouldn't do for his children – especially Lucy. He married again, to GP Beverly Marshall, but their marriage faltered when she became obsessed with having children. Jim patented a car jack that meant he could give up work, allowing him more time to spend with his family and neighbours. His biggest suprise came when a son he never knew he had concieved turned up on his doorstep and decided to stay. Despite being a good-looking, wealthy man, Jim dated relatively few women in the seven-and-a-half years he was on the street (Alan Dale, who played him, thought he was too celibate to be true!), but they included Zoe Davis, Caroline Alessi, Ruth Williams and Fiona Hartman – who conned him out of his money before his death in March 1994 of a heart attack.

Neighbours

It was good to have him around and he made a perfect replacement for Scott, who had long since moved to number 24 after marrying Charlene Mitchell. Jim had disapproved of his son's relationship with the girl next door, since he saw Charlene as a good-for-nothing tearaway. But Charlene proved to be the making of his younger son. Once they were together, they were less distracted and Scott was able to study hard and pass his HSC at the second time of trying. After that, it wasn't long before Scott left not just number 26, but Ramsay Street for good for a new life in Brisbane.

Helen wasn't nearly so lucky in love. The merry widow first thought she'd found love again in 1986 when a man posing as an art-world aficionado persuaded her that he could open an exhibition of her work and, as a keen amateur painter, this was a dream come true for Helen. But the dream turned into a nightmare when Douglas Blake was revealed to be a conman who had defrauded Helen of $40,000. It was only when Madge later conned Douglas that Helen retrieved some of her money. Helen did marry again though, to her late husband's cousin Michael Daniels. Perhaps predictably, it was never going to work out because Michael took her away from her family, so when it was revealed that Michael was still married to his first wife, the marriage was annulled on grounds of bigamy.

Helen was so much the focus of life at number 26 that it seemed strange when she moved out. She had brought so many waifs and strays into the home – including budding artist Nick Page, Hilary's illegitmate son Matt, and Todd's schoolmate Josh Anderson – and she was still so needed by the Robinsons.

The one who needed her most was Lucy. Perhaps, because she was the youngest, Lucy had been over-indulged, even spoiled, as a small child, but whatever else Lucy liked – and she liked most things – Lucy thrived on being the centre of attention. She was capricious and demanding, and changed her opinions and ambitions as frequently as the notorious Melbourne weather. Originally her ambition was to be a model, but when she decided she wanted to be a business hotshot, she demanded her dad send her to a private school. When she tired of that and

insisted that she return to Erinsborough High, Jim cowtowed to that too. It did mean things were getting tight at number 26, because another of Jim's children had recently come home to roost.

Glen Donnelly was Jim's son from a one-night stand he'd had with a nurse while serving in the Vietnam War. The girl he'd slept with had never contacted him to tell him she was pregnant, so the first Jim knew about Glen's existence was when he turned up on the doorstep asking for financial help towards his mother's funeral costs. Glen assumed that Jim had not wanted to know him and came in fight-picking mood. It took all of Jim's powers of diplomacy to convince Glen that the reason he'd never been in contact with him was because he hadn't even known about him, and in the end he was able to persuade Glen to stay. However, he asked Glen to keep his true identity a secret until he'd told his other kids himself.

But he didn't tell Lucy fast enough, and within days Lucy and Glen were unable to deny the attraction between them and the half brother and sister shared a passionate kiss. Only then did Jim come clean, and

HELEN DANIELS
Anne Haddy

Reg Watson created the part of Helen Daniels to dispel the myth that all mothers-in-law are battle-axes. Played by Anne Haddy, she is the only character to have stayed in the soap for all ten years. She is the linchpin of *Neighbours* and the person people turn to when they're in trouble. Her life of experience means she has words of comfort for every situation: she was happily married to Bill Daniels for over forty years, or so she thought. It was only after his death she learnt her sister Laura had had an affair with him. She also had the pain of burying one daughter (and bringing up her children) and telling the other that she was adopted. She married again twice, first to Bill's cousin Michael (but this was later annulled as he was revealed to be a bigamist) and to Ruben White who died shortly after the ceremony. Helen is everyone's friend and is universally loved.

Paul was furious at his father: not only had he been unfaithful to their mother, but he had allowed his illegitimate son to turn their family upside down. It was inevitable that Glen and Paul would come to blows, and Glen resented that the only jobs he could get meant his aggressive half brother would be his boss. Tragedy struck when Glen was repairing the roof of Lassiters Complex and fell, leaving him paralysed from the waist down.

Glen's girlfriend, Gaby Willis, was as supportive as she could be, but nothing could remove the chip on his shoulder the size of Ayer's Rock. Glen was convinced he would only ever be done wrong by the Robinsons and left Erinsborough for good.

Lucy was about to flee the nest again as well. After fighting with country girl Beth Brennan for surfer Brad Willis's affections, she was offered a modelling contract in Singapore. She didn't really want to leave Ramsay Street, but as modelling had been her childhood ambition, she couldn't turn the offer down and so she said a tearful goodbye to Helen, Jim and Brad and went off to start the endless whirl of catwalks and photographic assignments.

Now that number 26 was free of Robinson kids, it was time for Jim's elder daughter to return. Not much had been heard of from Julie, but she had married Philip and they'd had a daughter of their own called Hannah. The Martins returned to Ramsay Street on the sad occasion of Todd Landers' funeral. Todd had become like a son to Jim, so when the eighteen-year-old got his girlfriend, Phoebe Bright, pregnant, it was Jim he turned to for advice. As Phoebe prepared to have an abortion at a clinic, Todd confided in Jim that he really wanted the baby, and Jim encouraged him to go to the clinic before it was too late. But in his haste, Todd rushed across a busy road and was hit and killed by an oncoming van.

After the funeral, Julie revealed that things had not been going well for the Martins since Philip – now walking again! – had lost his job. Jim and Helen invited them and their children to stay at number 26 until they sorted themselves out, and Paul asked Philip to use his banking experience to run the show at Lassiters. It seemed they had landed on their feet, but trouble – as always – was right around the corner.

Philip's eldest child Michael had turned nasty from the minute Philip and Julie had got together. He blamed Julie for his mum's death and resented her trying to step into her shoes. He believed it was her seduction of Philip that had driven Loretta to drink, not Loretta's drinking that had led Philip to have an affair. So when he was released from a detention centre and came to live with his family, he made it his business to wreak as much havoc as possible – at one time he even tried to kill Julie by slowly poisoning her.

Just as Jim and Julie were getting to know each other again, Jim's character underwent a sea change. He started becoming evasive, curt and, at times, rude. Helen and Julie put the pieces together and decided he had started seeing a new woman, but they couldn't work out why he was keeping her a secret. Until they found out who it was: Annalise's scheming mother Fiona Hartman.

Julie and Helen had seen how Fiona operated and they couldn't believe Jim would be taken in by such a vixen, but he was and he was having none of their posturing. He was in love for the first time in years and he wasn't going to hear an unkind word said about the woman he intended to marry.

In protest, Helen and the Martins moved into number 32, which Helen had bought the previous year as an investment. But love didn't just make Jim blind to Fiona's true nature, it made him deaf to his family's pleadings. He went ahead and began living with Fiona and made plans for them to invest their money together in a new beauty salon. Jim signed over power of attorney of his accounts to Fiona.

But then tragedy struck. After playing with his granddaughter Hannah and her puppy Holly, Jim felt tight-chested and said he'd go home for a lie down. But as he came through the back door of number 26, he clasped his chest, collapsed and died of a heart attack. Fiona returned home later and found his body on the kitchen floor. She rushed to call an ambulance, but as the operator asked for her details she smiled and put the receiver back on its cradle: this was her chance to divert all of Jim's funds into her accounts.

She hurried to her bank and signed the necessary forms, only to return later, coincidentally at the same time as Rosemary to

Neighbours

'discover' the body for the first time. Fiona was an accomplished con artist and she even managed to convince the grieving Robinsons that she missed Jim too. It was only after his funeral that her dastardly deeds came to light, and Fiona did a runner before anyone could get their hands on the money.

Jim's death was a milestone in *Neighbours*' history. He and his family had been the focal point of the action for so long and he had seen many characters come and go during his years on the street. In his will, Jim left Helen a life tenancy of number 26 so that on her death Paul, Glen, Scott and Lucy would each inherit a quarter of the house. To Julie he left his half share in Lou's car yard, which he had bought as an investment. So Helen returned to number 26, filled as it was with so many happy and sad memories.

She rented one of the bedrooms to her cousin Thelma's son Wayne Duncan, who had moved to the neighbourhood to teach at Erinsborough high, and Annalise also moved in. The three of them lived together surprisingly well, the only real problems came when Wayne's girlfriend – and Annalise's arch enemy – Gaby Willis came round.

In the middle of the comparative calm, a bolt from the blue juddered through Helen's life. While packing up Jim's things, she stopped to read some of the love letters her daughter Anne and Jim had written to each other in the early days of their marriage – and they revealed some devastating information: Julie was not Jim's child. The letters revealed that Julie's natural father was one Roger Bannon, and Helen thought her granddaughter had a right to know the truth. Unsurprisingly, Julie was knocked sideways to learn that the man she had always called 'dad' wasn't her real father, but she was curious to know about Roger Bannon and she set about tracking him down. She discovered from his wife that he had died, but his wife also told Julie something much more disturbing – that she was a product of a rape. The revelation sent Julie into a tailspin and her confused behaviour was unfathomable by Philip. It

LUCY ROBINSON
Melissa Bell

In an attempt to make *Neighbours* appeal to all ages, Reg Watson included nine-year-old Lucy. When the show first started, Lucy was an innocent kid who got into scrapes but never did anything seriously wrong. She was packed off to boarding school at the age of eleven and returned to be played by a different actress. It was only when she was re-cast for a third time (and played by Melissa Bell) that Lucy became a central character as a teenager. She caused her dad no end of worry: she flitted from career to dead-end job, flirted with every man she met – including her half-brother Glen in scenes considered too risqué for UK audiences and were cut – and ended up leaving Erinsborough for the precarious world of modelling in Singapore, where she married her sleazy agent David Kazalian. Thankfully, Jim didn't live to see his daughter disgraced as a centrefold model and go-go dancer in her quest to become a covergirl.

led to them separating and Julie moved back into her old house.

But big reunions were to come. Helen was due for a birthday celebration and as many Robinsons as the neighbours could contact would be there. Paul and Lucy both came for the big day – it was the first time Lucy and Julie had appeared on screen together for seven years and both characters were now played by different actresses! – and Philip also turned up to hear Julie tell him the truth about why she

had been behaving so badly. He told her he didn't care about their past, only their future together. Helen declared that seeing Julie and Philip back together was her birthday wish come true.

While he was back in Erinsborough, Paul took the opportunity to go over the books at Lassiters. When Philip's assistant, Gaby, found Paul working late on some of Philip's personal files, her suspicions were aroused. She told Philip what she'd seen but he said he wasn't worried – after all,

HANNAH MARTIN
Rebecca Ritters

Of all the young characters to have appeared in *Neighbours*, Hannah has been one of the most endearing. In her years in the Street Hannah has seen her parents split up and get back together, and watched her mum die. All this trauma has meant Hannah has suffered from bed-wetting from time to time and various attention-seeking scams. Hannah grew up scared of her violent half-brother Michael, but always knew her doting dad Philip would protect her from harm. Philip indulged his youngest daughter, and his pet name for her was Button. As Hannah grew up and started to see boys as an attraction rather than the enemy, she found 'Button' babyish and insisted her dad call her by her proper name. After her mother, Julie, died, she was keen for her dad to find a replacement as soon as possible and never made a fuss about him dating other women – and when Jen Handley came along it was Hannah who begged her dad to see her again.

Paul was his brother-in-law and he wasn't going to hurt him, was he? But when the police came to arrest Philip the next day on fraud charges, Gaby realized she'd had good reason to be suspicious. Paul knew it wouldn't be long before the police would discover Philip was innocent, so he phoned Chrissie in Hawaii, told her to clear the joint account and meet him in Rio. And as Paul hastily made his way to

the airport in a taxi for his life as a fugitive, he handed a letter exonerating Philip to the cabbie with instructions to hand it over to the police.

Lucy was also to cause Helen heartache when she announced that her agent was coming to visit, and her agent announced he was her husband! Lucy was now Mrs David Kazalian and she was besotted. She claimed she owed all her success to him and that he would do anything for her. Helen and Julie were suspicious, however. There was something sleazy about Mr Kazalian and they just didn't trust him. But the impetuous Lucy had left them with no choice other than to welcome him into the family as her husband.

Lucy left Erinsborough not long after Helen's birthday party and she wasn't to return again until after her sister's death. Julie accidentally fell from a building in the summer of 1995, following which Philip and family moved back into number 26 to be with the grieving Helen. The Robinson/Martin clan didn't know Lucy had returned to Erinsborough until Mark Gottlieb spotted her dancing as a go-go dancer in a club. Mark and Lucy had once double dated when Lucy was trying to get Brad and Beth back together, so there was no mistake when he spotted her doing her act, even if she had cut off her locks and bleached what was left of her hair. Disgraced, Lucy was made to return to the family fold where Helen could keep an eye on her. And as Debbie Martin, who had recovered from her bulimia, had gone to live and work with Rosemary in New York, Lucy could even have her old bedroom back.

Helen, however, was making plans to move out. She had fallen passionately in love with a rich art lover called Reuben White (played by Anne Haddy's real-life husband who several years before had played another of Helen's lovers, Douglas Blake!). But Reuben suffered from a heart complaint that could threaten his life at any moment, so the couple vowed to live their lives to the full and take things one day at a time. Reuben and Helen wanted to marry, and even though Helen knew she might soon be widowed she desperately wanted to marry Reuben and move in with him. Only days after their elegant wedding Helen's new husband passed away peacefully while sitting in a chair in the sun, and so she moved back to number 26 to be with her family.

There was to be one more addition to number 26 and she was to become the new woman in Philip's life. Following Philip's period of mourning for Julie – which included being arrested for her murder until Debbie remembered what had actually happened the night of Julie's death – Philip embarked on the dating game. As he was more than a little out of touch, he had plenty of disastrous dates before one of Cody's friends from medical school decided Philip was the man for her. Jen Handley was a mature student, but because Cody was old for her years the two women got on famously. Even so, Cody was a little surprised when Jen declared her intentions towards Philip – after all there was quite an age gap and Philip had far more tummy than he did hair. But Jen was adamant, and she set out to seduce him. At first Philip thought she was just being kind, but when even Hannah told him to go for it, Philip let his inhibitions go and, before long, Jen had made number 26 her home.

Des Clarke may have been the respectable assistant manager at the local branch of the Pacific Bank, but his stag party in *Neighbours'* very first episode was anything but respectable. It was loud enough for Max Ramsay to complain even before the stripper arrived; but after pretty Daphne Lawrence had taken her clothes off, Max was ready to call the police. Instead, though, he went round to number 28 to end the celebrations in his own heavy-handed way. His intervention was too late, though, for news of the raucous bash had already filtered through to Des's prissy fiancée, Lorraine Kingham, who came round the next morning to call the afternoon's ceremony off. Her conviction that she had made the right decision was reinforced when she came face to face with the stripper who had returned to pick up some items she'd left behind in the Max-induced confusion. When Lorraine stormed off, Daphne quickly realized what had happened and offered to help Des pay the mortgage by renting a room off him. Bemused, Des accepted and the neighbours' dreams of having a respectable couple from the bank living in the street were shattered.

Des had previously dated Julie Robinson, who was horrified that she had once gone out with a social degenerate, for that's what he must be if could rent to a woman of such low morals. But the young men in the street were very pleased to have Daphne as a neighbour and they practically queued up to date her. It was Shane Ramsay who took her fancy and, at one point, she even suggested they move in together. Shane just wasn't ready for that sort of commitment and the audience started to realize that Daphne wasn't as outrageous as she seemed, and that all she really wanted was to get married and be a mum. All along, the man she would eventually marry had been waiting quietly in the wings – her landlord Des. 'I do believe the landlord is flirting with the tenant,' was how she confronted Des. 'I do believe the tenant is enjoying it,' he responded. As everything moves at breakneck speed in Ramsay Street, it was only a matter of a month or so before Des popped the question, and naturally Daphne accepted.

On the morning of the wedding, Des became so sure that a fantastic girl like Daphne wouldn't marry him that it took his best man, Paul, all his powers of persuasion to get him to the altar. There was slightly more difficulty getting the bride to altar because she was being held hostage by a bank robber! When Daphne didn't turn up on time, Des was convinced he'd been jilted and ran off. It was only when he returned to Ramsay Street a few days later that he discovered the truth and the nuptials were re-scheduled and went like clockwork.

Des and Daphne were not to have their house to themselves for long, as Daphne's best friend, Zoe Davis, invited herself to stay – partly to check that her go-getting friend was all right after marrying such a boring man – and Daphne also took pity on local teenager, Mike Young, who was being beaten by his father and she asked him to live with them.

Things ran smoothly for the residents of number 28: Daphne's doting granddad, Harry Henderson, bought her the Coffee Shop in the local Lassiters complex, Des got promoted to manager and both Mike and Zoe found love. Mike took up with Jane Harris, Mrs Mangel's granddaughter

from number 32, and Zoe shocked the neighbourhood by luring older man Jim Robinson into bed. Jim's children, especially Lucy, weren't happy at the prospect of another woman in Jim's life, but when Zoe announced she was pregnant they had to get used to the idea. Just a couple of days later, though, she miscarried and the trauma of losing the baby drove Jim and Zoe apart. Zoe decided to leave Erinsborough.

That wasn't the only pregnancy in the street. When Des started getting cravings for pickled chillies with ice cream, neighbourly doctor Clive Gibbons diagnosed that he was having sympathetic pregnancy cravings, and that, after months of trying, Daphne was at last expecting.

When the baby arrived, typically for the ever dramatic *Neighbours*, it was not on time or in a maternity ward. No, baby Clarke decided to make his presence felt when his parents were enjoying a picnic. Jim Robinson and his doctor fiancée, Beverly Marshall, had gone on the picnic too but were taking a walk when the contractions started. Des had to be midwife as the baby was coming fast and there was no time to get to the hospital. But, just in the nick of time, Beverly and Jim came back for the expert to handle the delivery.

The next drama of course was naming the boy. Des's interfering mother Eileen wanted him to have her maiden name, Kingsley, but the Clarkes plumped for Jamie which allowed Jim, who was at the birth, and Mike, whose middle name was James, to claim that the tot had been named after them. Both men were asked to be godfathers.

Things couldn't have been going better for the Clarkes, but into every life a drop

DOUG WILLIS
Terence Donovan

Doug was a bit of a Regular Joe. He didn't like rocking the boat or standing out from the crowd, he just liked to get a decent day's pay for a decent day's work. Played by Jason Donovan's real-life father, he owned his own construction firm and hoped one day to pass it on to one of his sons, but neither showed any enthusiasm for the builder's life (except for when Adam tried to prove to his father that he was man enough to do the job). After a difficult relationship with his dad, Bert, Doug was determined always to be around for his four kids, and the only time he did anything to hurt his family was when he succumbed to the temptations Jill Weir made every effort to put in his way. Doug could easily be described as a man's man; he was never afraid to use his fists and one of his greatest pleasures was making home-brewed beer with his best mate, Lou.

of rain must fall – only for the Clarkes it was monsoon season. Daphne's father, from whom she'd been estranged for several years, fell ill and wanted to make peace with his daughter before he died. Once she had seen her father, Daphne's unbounding compassion led her to the decision that she would tend to him in his final weeks. This storyline was introduced as a way of writing out the popular Daphne without killing her off. But the fans demanded a more resolved conclusion and so, on the way to Mr Lawrence's funeral, Daphne's car crashed. She was rushed to hospital where she survived in a coma for weeks while producers negotiated with actress Elaine Smith to bring the character back. Smith was adamant she

wanted out, though, and so Daphne only woke up long enough to say 'I love you, Clarkey' before slipping away.

Des never really recovered from losing Daphne, both because he never found anyone to replace her and also because the scriptwriters were a little lost as to what to do with him. They gave him a nanny, Bronwyn Davies, who eventually married Henry Ramsay, and a couple of dead-end affairs (one somewhat unbelievably with Jane Harris) before he sold up and moved to Perth, leaving the keys of number 28 in the hands of the Willis family.

Cody Willis was already familiar to viewers as Todd Landers' studious girlfriend, so the Willis family slipped into Ramsay Street with ease. Doug Willis,

PAM WILLIS
Sue Jones

A real salt-of-the-earth type, Pam could always be relied on to help out especially if it benefitted one of her four children. Pam worked as a nurse at the local hospital, and her medical duties often got her involved in difficult situations. The most difficult was when one of her home visits, an old man named Garth Kirby, asked her to give him something that would send him to sleep forever. She refused, but the next time she called on Garth she found him dead and was promptly arrested for his murder, although the medical evidence later exonerated her. Pam was given an old motorbike by Penelope, a friend of hers in her sixties, who had a stroke and could no longer use her legs fully –

something that made her biker nephew Cameron jealous. She now lives in Darwin with her husband where she keeps a close eye on her daughter, Gaby, and Gaby's son, Zac.

an affable fortysomething, was a self-employed builder who loved his family and enjoyed a drink or two with his mates. His wife of many years, Pam, had spent the last twenty of them at home as a full-time mother looking after their four kids: Adam, a medical student; Gaby, currently on a business course in Japan; Brad, in America on a basketball scholarship; and Cody, the youngest. But now that there was only Cody still at school, Pam – an even-keeled coper – wanted to return to nursing. Doug was appalled at the thought of his wife working again. Apart from the fact he liked the idea of providing for her, there was the small question of who would provide his meals – but Pam was determined and studied hard to re-qualify. In time she did, and found a post at the local hospital.

Pam's job gave her good reason to get involved in people's lives; she was either at the hospital when they were admitted or they turned to her for advice, and she became a trusted and central figure in the community. It was obvious that her kids were only passing through, however. Adam was bright and it was clear that he would one day flee the nest, but not before wooing several of his female neighbours. The one who initially caught his eye was Caroline Alessi. There was a certain disparity between her high-flying income and his student grant, but she fell for his genuine charm and cute looks. But when Jim Robinson started showing an interest in Caroline, Adam was dropped quicker than you can say didgeridoo. He found lasting love, though, with Madge's niece, Gemma Ramsay. Like many other Ramsay Street teenagers, Adam and Gemma confounded the odds by making a go of

things. So when Gemma got a posting to an animal sanctuary in Newcastle, New South Wales, Adam switched his medical degree to a university in Newcastle to be with her.

Cody, too, was set to move on. As a bright student she was put forward by head teacher Dorothy Burke for a scholarship to study in America. Cody didn't really want to go – for at the time she was deeply involved with Todd Landers – but when the news came through that she had got one of the coveted places, she and Todd agreed it was too good an opportunity to turn down. They said a tearful farewell and pledged to stay faithful, but within months she had written to him to say she needed space. It wasn't until she returned a couple of years later that we found out why.

The Willis children's rooms were not left empty for long, for Gaby returned from Japan and Brad also tried to make it home but was stopped in the (fictional) country of Bahgee for drug trafficking. In Bahgee the penalty, if found guilty, was death and so, panicked, Doug and Pam flew to Bahgee in the hope of returning with their younger son.

Things didn't look good, but when they arrived back in Melbourne they did indeed have Brad with them and brother and sister had an emotional meeting after years apart.

Brad had always been intended to be a basketball pro by the scriptwriters, but when they offered the part to the actor he said thanks very much but, hey, I surf. And so Brad became a surf bum and on his very first morning in Erinsborough he got up before the sun to be at the beach for the first set of the day; it was clear that

Brad was not going to be a high achiever like his siblings.

Both Gaby and Brad were to have many love affairs in Ramsay Street, but their parents' marriage was about to face its toughest test. When Doug's photo was printed in the *Erinsborough News*, a woman named Jill Weir saw the article, fell in love with him and resolved to make him hers. So serious was she that she realized the best friend she could make would be Pam. She courted the Willis's friendship and when she was alone with Doug she made no bones about her intentions, but as soon as Pam was around she was as sweet as pie. Doug didn't tell his wife about Jill's ulterior motive in case it caused her distress, but when he returned home one day to find Pam had offered Jill a room after she'd been made homeless, he wished he'd said something before.

At the same time, Pam had found herself spending a lot of time with Jim Robinson, so much time in fact that he found himself falling in love with her. Pam was so committed to her marriage that she didn't see the opportunity for an affair that was right in front of her eyes – but Doug did, and he became convinced his wife was sleeping with his best mate.

So when Jill followed Doug to an upstate convention he was attending and offered herself to him, he didn't refuse. Gaby meanwhile caught her mother in a passionate embrace with Jim and feared her mum and dad were heading for the divorce courts.

Doug returned, guilt-ridden, from his conference and confessed to his adultery while accusing Pam of the same crime. Pam was wounded on both counts; one that he had been unfaithful; and two that he obviously didn't trust her. It was war. Gaby tried her best to play peacemaker but she was told to keep her nose out, and all she could do was let her parents fight it out. Both Pam and Doug were prepared for a long battle and to use whatever it took to win.

Brad was too laid-back to take sides or get involved, and he was far too busy falling in love and finding work. At first he made his money making surfboards in the garage, but after some of his designs got ripped off he decided it would be safer working for somebody else and took a job at The Waterhole. His love life, however, was a little more complicated. When he and some of the other youngsters from the street went on holiday in Queensland – where the surf is better, of course – he realized he was attracted to neighbour Lucy Robinson, but also found himself fancying a girl he met in the resort, Beth Brennan. Beth and Lucy were willing to fight for Brad, and in the end Lucy won. But only the battle, not the war – for Beth was about to follow the Ramsay Street crew back to Erinsborough and maintain her quest for Brad.

Lucy and Brad were a pretty solid item though, and it took Lucy's departure for a modelling career in Singapore for Beth to get a look in. And even then she had to beg Brad. After being teased by Annalise for being a virgin, Beth was desperate to unburden herself of her innocence. So she asked Brad if he would oblige, but his opinion was that it was such an important thing that she should wait until she fell in love with someone, because the first time should be special. But Beth already had fallen in love with someone – him – and when they were trapped alone on a building site they were guarding for Doug, they made love for the first time. It wasn't long before Brad put an engagement ring on her finger.

Gaby was also getting engaged. She had fallen for Jim's illegitimate son, Glen Donnelly, who had been a great support to her while she'd been setting up her own clothing boutique called Gabrielle. Gaby had always had a knack with a sewing machine and after several of the neighbours had asked her to make things for them, Gaby, ever the businesswoman, decided to use her skill for profit and rented a shop in the Lassiters complex. It had been Glen's suggestion to capitalize on her client with a famous name – one Elizabeth Taylor – to get publicity in the *Erinsborough News* and it worked a treat: Gaby's profits started to climb.

But tragedy was close at hand. While Glen tried to fix a banner to the roof of the Lassiters complex he fell and was paralysed from the waist down. His fiancée vowed to help him, but his pride was hurt almost as much as his body, and he decided to leave Erinsborough and was never heard from again. Gaby was not to be on her own for long though, as another estranged relative of the Robinsons – Helen's cousin's son – was about to grab her attention. There was a real chemistry between Gaby and her new beau, school teacher Wayne Duncan, but that was just about it. They were about as mis-matched as you could get: Gaby enjoyed the cinema, Wayne liked camping; Gaby liked spending time with her family, Wayne enjoyed bike riding, or horse riding – or just about anything that had next to no appeal for Gaby. But they couldn't get each other out of their minds and kept on coming together for sparring sessions. In the end they had to force themselves to keep apart from each other because they realized how destructive their relationship was. Of course, Gaby's cascading dark hair and model's looks meant there was never a shortage of men after her. But some of the attention was most definitely unwanted. Once she had landed the job of number two at Lassiters, she had a brief association with a client of the hotel's called Simon Hunter. But when they went away for the weekend he tried to rape her, and then he (successfully) bribed her into not pressing charges. Characteristically, she turned the experience into a positive and set about furthering her career. She also decided she wanted to get her pilot's licence.

Doug and Pam's stalemate continued for months, and it wasn't until Doug was missing at sea after a fishing expedition that Pam realized she still really loved him, and that whatever he had done wrong it was not worth throwing away her marriage over it. So when Doug was returned to shore by the coastguard she told him she loved him and they reunited. They also had something to celebrate; Brad and Beth's imminent nuptials. Beth had asked Gaby to make her wedding gown and the bridesmaids' dresses, which she did with pleasure for her future sister-in-law in her free evenings. But while the Willises and Beth were occupying themselves with wedding plans, Brad's mind was elsewhere. He had become involved with Lou Carpenter's daughter, Lauren, and no matter how hard they tried to stop themselves, they just couldn't. Beth had her suspicions that Brad was seeing someone else, but it wasn't until the morning of the wedding that she realized it was her bridesmaid!

So as the minister asked her if she took Brad to be her lawfully wedded husband she replied that she didn't and fled. She left Ramsay Street for a while to get over it, leaving Brad free to date Lauren openly. But like Gaby and Wayne's relationship, Lauren and Brad's was also based on lust, and in time they came to acknowledge this. And when Beth returned to Ramsay Street it was abundantly clear that she was still very much in love with Brad as was he with her – he'd let lust lead him astray.

As well as finding it hard to trust Brad again, Beth had another worry; as Doug's apprentice at Willis Construction she was about to lose her job, as a tax debt forced Doug to sell out to a big conglomerate. He did all he could to secure an apprenticeship for Beth in the new company as he had come to think of Beth like a daughter during her relationship with his son. But not many building companies were keen to take on a girl as an apprentice and the only post they could find for her was thousands of miles away in Perth. The thought of Beth being so far away was too much for Brad and so he asked her to marry him again, and she accepted. Family and neighbours were so excited that these two were finally going to tie the knot that they swamped them with plans and arrangements – so much so that the happy couple started to feel like it was no longer their wedding. They decided to elope and, after a quick registrar's office service they planned to get on the bus to Perth and only tell the rest of the Willises what they'd done when they got to Western Australia.

The rest of the family had gone full steam ahead with their own plans, but had forgotten one vital ingredient – the bride and groom! When someone said they'd seen them at the bus depot, Pam and Doug got in the car and headed out of town to try and catch the bus. They eventually flagged it down and dragged Brad and Beth back to Ramsay Street for their second wedding! But then it really was goodbye to two of *Neighbours'* best-loved lovers as they left after the wedding for another bus to Perth!

Just before Brad departed, however, his little sister Cody called to say she was on her way home. Pam and Doug were thrilled to have three of their kids under one roof at one time, even if was only going to be for a couple of weeks. As soon as Cody stepped through the front door of number 28 it was clear she was a changed person (and not just because the character had been re-cast!). She was clearly broken-hearted, and still carrying a torch for the man who'd done the breaking. But there were plenty of lads around who were willing to take her mind off things, notably Rick Alessi and Michael Martin. Although there was an immediate attraction between her and Rick, he was about to leave Ramsay Street and so she became involved with Michael – but only until Rick returned! They were made for each other; they had the same sense of humour, were both ambitious – albeit in very different ways – and were both crazy about each other. There was just one problem; Cody was married.

When a handsome American arrived in Ramsay Street asking for Cody, he caught everybody's eye, but he only had eyes for her. He tracked her down, but it was clear from the expression on Cody's face that she was not pleased to see him, partly because she hadn't told her folks that she was in fact Mrs Drew Grover, but mostly because he had treated her very badly. Cody had married him because she was young and thought she loved him. He had been keen to marry her because his company would benefit from his having Australian residency, and his political ambitions would be more easily achieved if he had a pretty wife by his side. Conversely, his political career could be damaged if he had a divorce to explain to the voters. And so he came to persuade Cody to come back to him. She refused point blank and, being the assertive sort, she stood her ground until he left for America and the divorce proceedings had started.

Her big sister Gaby, however, was flying high – literally. Not only was she close to qualifying for her pilot's licence, but she was also smitten with her flying instructor, Jack Flynn. She had also got the job she wanted at Lassiters. After Philip and Julie's marriage had hit the rocks and Philip disappeared, Paul gave Gaby the top job. When Philip returned he was re-instated. Philip, however, was soon to grow disillusioned with the corporate world and quit, leaving Gaby in charge. When Cheryl Stark bought the complex the two women clashed over how it should be run and Gaby looked around for work elsewhere and found it – in the fashion industry in Greece. And so she made plans to leave her family and start a new life in Greece.

Pam and Doug feared they'd seen the last of their daughter for some time, but tears of joy were shed when she unexpectedly returned a few months later, although she wouldn't tell them why. She reapplied for her old job at Lassiters, but when she felt she was being dismissed by her interviewers because she was a woman, she blew up at them and told them another reason they wouldn't want to give her the job was because she was pregnant and they wouldn't want to pay her maternity leave! They were so impressed by her feistyness that they gave her the job!

But now she had to ask her parents if they wanted to be called grandma and grandpa or nan and granddad! Naturally, Pam and Doug were shocked to learn their elder daughter was pregnant out of wedlock, especially as she hadn't even told them who the father was – and didn't intend to. But when they got their calendar out they worked out it must be Jack, the flying instructor. Doug was quick to give Jack a hiding for taking his responsibilities lightly, but Gaby had decided not to tell Jack.

Once Jack had been told he was going to be a father though, he took his responsibilities seriously and offered to help Gaby financially, as it was clear she wanted to raise her child by herself. Gaby felt people didn't think she could cope but recognized Jack's rights and they agreed he could see the baby as often as he wanted.

The baby arrived – on the same day as Cheryl and Lou's daughter Louise – and it was a boy. Gaby, determined that she wasn't going to do things the conventional way, wanted to give her son a more unusual name than any her family were

THE KENNEDY FAMILY

Alan Fletcher,
Jackie Woodburne,
Benji McNair,
Kym Valentine,
Jesse Spencer

At a time when it seemed as though every house in Ramsay Street was populated by assorted misfits and distant relatives, the storyliners introduced the solid Kennedy family to take *Neighbours* back to its roots. And in making Karl Kennedy the local GP and his wife, Susan, a teacher at the local school, they were ideally placed to have a finger immediately in most of their neighbours' pies. The Kennedy children quickly got equally involved in Ramsay Street shenanigans: Mal moved in to number 32 to live with his girlfriend Danni Stark; Libby made a stand on any and every issue; and Billy became good friends with Hannah Martin from next door. Karl often gets frustrated by his wife's good nature and his daughter's political views (she is a Communist) because all he really wants is for things to run smoothly – and for his dinner to be on the table when he expects it to be there.

considering, and he was named Zac. Gaby tried to balance being a mum and running Lassiters but in the end she had to accept defeat, and so she took a less stressful job in Darwin.

Pam and Doug also felt their time in Erinsborough was over, and thought they might move to Darwin too so they could dote on their first grandchild. Cody, on the other hand, had different plans. There was no way she was willing to kiss goodbye to the good thing she had going with Rick, especially when she was working so hard to follow her big brother Adam into medicine. So an arrangement was reached that Cody would move in with Helen Daniels, who would keep her on the straight and narrow, and Pam and Doug would make the break for Darwin.

Number 28 was then bought by Karl and Susan Kennedy, who moved in in 1995 with their children Malcolm, Libby and Billy. Karl is a traditional guy who knows what he likes and wants only what he likes. Susan, his childhood sweetheart, is a bit more open minded, which comes in handy when she deals with the kids at Erinsborough High, where she teaches. Mal, their eldest, found himself immediately attracted to Danni Stark and the two embarked on a passionate relationship and were inseparable. Typically, their parents disapproved, but the two teenagers were determined to be together, so they rented number 32 where they had their privacy but their parents could still keep an eye on them.

Libby, an opinionated girl who has things to say on most subjects from communism to environmentalism, still lives at home with her mum and dad, as does the youngest of the clan, Billy.

NUMBER
30

The first time Number 30 was used in *Neighbours* was when Jim Robinson rented it for his eldest son Paul and his first wife Terri in 1987. But they had barely moved in before the cracks in their marriage turned into chasms and Terri shot Paul in the shoulder in an attempt to stop him shopping her to the police.

From when they moved out in 1987 until 1991, when school principal Dorothy Burke moved in, the house wasn't seen on screen. Dorothy was haughty and her severe looks and quirky personality (she was never seen without her parasol on a bright day) meant the pupils who lived in the street were fearful of her. But, as with most of *Neighbours'* more prickly characters, Dorothy eventually showed everyone her softer side when her niece and nephew Lochie and Ryan came to live with her. Lochie had been great friends with Toby Mangel; his mum Kerry used to childmind Lochie for Dorothy. When Kerry died, Lochie had to return to her parents as there was no one to look after her, but as Ryan was at school he stayed on so his studies weren't interrupted.

Dorothy had always maintained that she was a widow, but Ryan soon discovered that this was just a story to hide her shame. In a drawer he found letters from his uncle Colin with some of the sentences cut out, something he knew happened to correspondence from prison inmates. He confronted his aunt with his theory that her husband was in jail – and she couldn't deny it. Colin had abused his position as an accountant to commit a major fraud, and in doing so embarrassed his school-principal wife to the point where she denied his existence.

When Colin was released he immediately turned to Dorothy for support – and a roof over his head and food to eat. Although Dorothy was reluctant, he turned on the charm and wheedled his way round her. To her surprise she also found herself falling for him again, and falling for his 'reformed character' protestations. But when Joe Mangel was cleaning the windows at Lassiters he spied Colin in one of the hotel rooms with Rosemary Daniels, who had no idea Colin was married. Dorothy threw him out the very same day.

Ryan got a lot of stick at school because of his aunt; it was bad enough that she was the principal, but that she was so weird too made it hard for him. Dorothy was very well travelled and number 30 was filled with tribal masks and spears as well as artefacts from around the world, so when Ryan brought schoolfriends home they were even more convinced their principal was off her rocker.

It was enough to drive Ryan round the twist and, predictably, he rebelled against her authoritarianism – and joined the army! But Dorothy was not to be on her own for long. When Joe and Melanie Mangel went to England for their honeymoon they left Toby in Dorothy's charge, and when they decided to stay in England, Toby stayed at number 30. Dorothy also offered a room to one of her most promising students, Phoebe Bright, after her father's death had started to affect her grades. Phoebe came with one major drawback though – her pet snake Oscar! No wonder the other kids from school called her creepy Phoebe.

Phoebe's story was certainly an ugly-duckling tale. None of the boys in the street looked twice at her, hiding behind her nerdy spectacles and sensible shoes.

But once they got to know this sparky oddball they were charmed by her and both Todd and Josh fell for her. Phoebe only had eyes for Todd though, and the two of them became one of the most devoted couples in Ramsay Street.

Like most young couples, it wasn't long before they wanted to start experimenting with sex, but in their haste and inexperience they forgot to use contraception properly and Phoebe became pregnant. Both Todd and Phoebe were sensitive young adults who took their position as prospective parents seriously, and while they carefully considered keeping the baby, they both felt they wouldn't be able to provide the child with all the things it would need. So they decided that Phoebe would have an abortion, even though it was clear that neither of them wanted her to. On the day that Phoebe was due at the abortion clinic Todd moped around number 26 and it was obvious he felt they'd made the wrong decision. In a dramatic sequence he rushed to the clinic to stop Phoebe from having the operation, but was tragically run over. Jim managed to get word to the clinic before Phoebe entered the operating theatre and she and Dorothy rushed to the hospital where Todd was being treated, only to watch him die of a massive heart attack.

When Phoebe was told why Todd had been in such a hurry to get to the clinic there was no way she was going through with the operation, and she began preparing to be a single mum, albeit with plenty of help from Dorothy who had come to think of Phoebe and Toby as her own.

In her grief, Phoebe claimed that Todd had come to her in a vision and told her that she would have a daughter. No one, of course, believed her and assumed that the grief had affected her brain.

Phoebe's luck was about to change, however. While she was visiting Todd's grave she was approached by a young man who was also in mourning for his lover who had been killed in a car crash. The two had much in common and became instant friends. In fact they fitted into each other's lives so well that her new beau, record-store employee Stephen Gottlieb, proposed marriage – and Phoebe accepted.

After a brief courtship they made plans for a wedding, but they were all for nought when the baby Phoebe was carrying arrived prematurely the night before the ceremony. She gave birth to a daughter, and this convinced her that Todd really had come to her and was looking after them and approved of her marrying Stephen. As the tiny baby's life held in the balance, they named her Hope and they prayed she'd be fit enough to leave hospital for the rescheduled wedding a couple of weeks later.

As she was premature, Hope had a lot of problems and Phoebe and Stephen had to accept that she probably wouldn't be well enough in time. But just before the service started, neighbour and local nurse Pam turned up with a special wedding present – Hope.

Phoebe wasn't the only resident of number 30 to have found love unexpectedly: when education inspector Tom Merrick checked up on Erinsborough High he'd also checked out the principal! Although he was younger than Dorothy, these two odd-balls were well matched and before long he had whisked Dorothy off her feet and on to his motorbike and taken her – and Toby – off to live in the country with him.

Dorothy rented the house to the Gottliebs, but they needed someone else to help them pay the rent and advertised for a lodger. When Russell Butler saw Phoebe put up an ad in the Coffee Shop, which she and Stephen were now managing for Cathy Alessi, he took it down before anyone else had a chance to read it. He liked the look of Phoebe and he wanted to get to know her properly.

He turned up at the house to meet the Gottliebs formally, and even though Stephen didn't really take to him, as he was the only person who had replied to their ad, they let him move in. Unsurprisingly, it was only a matter of days before Russell started unsettling his flatmates. He would not pay his rent for weeks on end and then would suddenly hand the Gottliebs everything he owed just before they kicked him out. He put a lock on his door and banned them from entering his room, and whenever he was alone with Phoebe he would make lurid suggestions, but whenever Stephen was around he was chummy.

It transpired that Russell's ex-girlfriend had recently given birth to his child but because of his aggressive behaviour had banned him from seeing the baby. In Russell's eyes, Phoebe and Hope were perfect substitutes. The nightmare situation climaxed with Russell stealing Hope (although she was later returned safely) and Stephen asked Lou to send the heavies round to teach Russell a lesson. Unfortunately, the bovver boys mistook Wayne Duncan for Russell and it was Wayne who needed medical attention. The message got through to Russell though, and before his psychiatrist could find him a residential care place, he shot through.

The Gottliebs still needed help with the rent as the Coffee Shop didn't quite make enough money, and so Beth Brennan moved in. Things seemed to be looking up for the young couple, but tragedy was about to strike: Stephen was paralysed down one side when he was caught in an explosion at The Waterhole and he was left in a wheelchair. Just as he started to make some progress along the road to recovery, the arrival of his estranged brother, Mark (who

BETH BRENNAN
Natalie Imbruglia

Country girl Beth first came into *Neighbours* when she was holidaying with her brother, David, at the same resort as some of the Ramsay Street residents in Queensland. After being abused by her step-father, she fled to Ramsay Street to find solace with her new-found friends. She was instantly attracted to Brad Willis but had to wait until his girlfriend, Lucy Robinson, left town before she got him. They planned to marry, but Brad had an affair with her best friend Lauren, and Beth – a principled and sweet-natured girl – called it off at the last minute. Beth continued to work for Brad's dad as a builder's apprentice, but when Doug had to sell up the new owners of the building firm cancelled her apprenticeship. While Beth looked around for a new job, she fell back in love with Brad and they finally married in 1995 before moving to Perth where Beth had found a company which would take on a female apprentice.

had got the job of head chef at Lassiters after posing as a Frenchman called Marcel), sent him into a relapse. Stephen blamed his older brother for his former fiancée's death, and it was clear Mark had a lot of ground to make up if he was to build bridges with his brother and be a part of his niece's life.

The night Stephen's fiancée Libby had died, all three of them had been at a party together. Stephen had had to leave early and had arranged for his brother to drive Libby home. But when Mark got too drunk to drive, Libby was forced to take a cab which crashed, killing her instantly.

It was to be conversations about their unusual childhoods that finally brought Mark and Stephen eye to eye after so many years. Their parents had been hippies (Mark's real name was actually Cosmic!) and they and their sister had been brought up in a string of communes. Both of them resented their parents for what they saw as their backward ways.

In time, Stephen recovered from his injuries and he and Phoebe decided to move away from Erinsborough when he was offered a job at a record store in Anson's Corner.

Mark was ready to take over not just the lease on the house, but also the lease on the Coffee Shop. He was soon joined at the house by his girlfriend, Annalise, and Rick Alessi, who moved out of number 24 when the Starks moved in. From now on, number 30 became a mecca for lost souls and always seemed to take the rejects from the rest of the houses in the street.

Living with Mark and Annalise made Rick think seriously about love, and he ended up making a fool of himself over Gaby's friend Sally Pritchard who started teaching at the school, before he found his soul mate in Cody. Mark and Annalise, who was now managing the Coffee Shop, turned their thoughts to marriage. Ever one for thinking appearance matters, Annalise was determined to have a wedding worthy of a photo spread in a bridal magazine. But as Mark and his bride-to-be went through the interviews with the local priest to check their suitability, Mark started to question the sincerity of their commitment and started to think about what God really meant to him. Annalise was too busy with wedding preparations to notice her man was having doubts, and in fact it wasn't until Mark was in the church wearing his morning suit that his doubts got the better of him and, as Annalise came down the aisle, he met her halfway and told her the wedding was off. And as if that wasn't shocking enough, he then announced he intended to become a priest!

Obviously they could no longer live together after something like that, so Annalise moved in to number 24 after Sam Kratz told her how he felt about her. She was replaced at number 30 by Mark's flame-haired sister, Serendipity, or Ren for short. Serendipity was one of life's free spirits who was ruled by the heart rather than the head, and she brought a breath of fresh air into her brother's life. They had recently lost their mother to cancer and it was a good time for them to be together. And Ramsay Street was a great place to be for Ren as love was about to come her way in the shape of Jen Handley's younger brother, Luke, who had already moved into number 30. And as Rick had moved on to attend a hotel management course in America, there was room in the house. But their next flatmate wasn't exactly the type they were looking for.

Colin Taylor, the precise and annoying manager of the local newsagency was looking for a room, and although his tales of his

MARK GOTTLIEB
Bruce Samazan

When a top French chef applied for a job at Lassiters, managers Gaby and Philip were so excited they even prepared a special advertising campaign to flag their authentic cuisine. But it turned out that Marcel was actually Mark, who had faked his nationality and his accent so he could be near his estranged brother, Stephen, who had disowned him after Mark caused his girlfriend's death. But Stephen and Mark shared a strong bond due to their unusual childhood in a string of communes with hippie parents, and Stephen learned to forgive Mark. After moving in to number 30, Mark was instantly attracted to Annalise Hartman and when they had lived together for almost a year and successfully run the Coffee Shop between the two of them, they decided to marry. But in preparing for the church service Mark felt hypocritical that they were just using God to suit them, and he called off the service at the last minute, declaring his intention of becoming a priest. He started to lose friends with his holier-than-thou attitude, but a bump to the head soon brought him back to his senses.

REN GOTTLIEB

Raelee Hill

Serendipity first arrived in Ramsay Street to be with her brother, Mark, after the death of their mother. Unlike her brothers, Ren had thrived on the hippie communes of their childhood and was still a spiritual sort who believed in the healing properties of crystals and rebirth. But when she became involved with Danni Stark's fashion business, seeing to the PR for Danni's designs, the power went to her head. She started driving a BMW and at one point it looked like she was turning into Paul Robinson! But when she had a big bust-up with Danni she realized there were more important things in life than profit – like Luke Handley. Luke had been blasé about his relationship with Ren until she called his bluff and made him prove his love for her. While she was tending Mark in hospital after his fall, he proposed. When Luke was offered a job in Japan, Ren had to make her mind up if her future really was with him – and they left for the airport in May 1996.

CODY WILLIS
Peta Brady

Cody was the first of the Willises to arrive in Ramsay Street – when she dated Josh and then Todd – and she was the last to leave. Always a studious girl, when a scholarship place to study in America became available, she jumped at the chance. Cody returned two years later and went to finish her schooling at Erinsborough High where she was voted school captain. After a brief liaison with Michael Martin, she found herself falling deeply in love with one of her best friends, Rick Alessi, despite the fact that she had actually married in America. Her husband turned up after a few months to ask her to return, but she told him she only wanted a divorce. After her parents moved to Darwin, Cody lived at number 26, then 24 and finally 30 so she could carry on studying to be a doctor at the local medical college.

travels in China and his head crammed full of unusual facts bugged Mark and co. half to death, they felt a bit sorry for him and gave him a key to the house anyway. Colin was soon to move in on the Coffee Shop too, as well as in on Marlene Kratz.

Colin was one of the few people who agreed with Mark's sentiments in becoming a man of the cloth, but almost everyone else found Mark's new holier-than-thou stance unbearable and he started to lose many of his friends as he tried to ram his ideas down their throats. Even Ren found it hard to live with her brother at times, until a fall brought Mark to his senses and left him temporarily wheelchair-bound.

When Luke was offered a job in Japan, Ren had to make up her mind about whether she would follow him. And once she had decided their love was stronger than anything else, she packed her bags with glee. The day Mark said goodbye to 'Dippy' – his pet name for his little sister – was also the day that Cody Willis moved in after she'd had enough of living with Jo at number 24.

N U M B E R
32

The original resident of number 32 was Erinsborough's answer to the wicked witch of the West – Mrs Mangel. The shrew-like lady infuriated everyone she came across and some of the younger children were even afraid of her. If ever there was an opportunity to put a damper on something, she seized it with relish, and if ever there was a wrong deed committed, Mrs Mangel (nobody got to call her Nell), was already on the phone to report it to the police, the school or the parent concerned.

She claimed she lived with her husband, Len, and although she was heard shouting to him, he wasn't seen in Ramsay Street until 1994 when he turned up at a property Doug Willis was renovating. Helen Daniels recognized him and he tried to add her to his list of numerous conquests.

It was well known that Len was a philanderer – although Nell naturally denied that her marriage was anything other than perfect – and in fact many of the neighbours thought he had left her years ago and that she was just trying to save face. It was a mark of how vehemently Mrs Mangel was hated that even the most righteous person in the street couldn't blame Len for looking elsewhere. Eventually Mrs Mangel admitted that Len had finally left her, and that meant trouble for the residents of Ramsay Street – now she had even more time to have a go at them!

In 1987 her granddaughter Jane Harris moved in with her after her mother (Nell's daughter) moved to Hong Kong. Jane's nickname at school was Plain Jane the Superbrain, and indeed she was plain in her geeky glasses and was easily the brightest girl in the street. But Scott, Mike and Charlene soon found themselves becoming friends with Jane if only because she let them copy her homework. Charlene and Daphne, though, did see another side to Jane, looking beyond her grades and her glasses, and when they discovered that she had a crush on Mike they pledged they would do all they could to help her win his love.

Through careful planning on Charlene's part it was engineered that the only date Mike could get for a school dance was Jane. He thought he was going to be laughed at for taking the class swot, but when she turned up without glasses in a dress selected by Daphne with her hair and face done, Mike swooned and realized his date had beauty as well as brains.

Jane's change in appearance was strongly disapproved of by her uptight grandmother, but the confidence her new look gave her meant Jane could stand up to the old bag – the glasses and braids were gone forever.

Like most of the Ramsay Street residents, both Nell and Jane ended up working at the Lassiters complex. Nell got the job as housekeeper while her granddaughter ditched her numerous university offers to become Paul's secretary at the Robinson Corporation. Needless to say, they were both fastidious in their work. Nell had finally found a good use for her meticulous, by-the-book nature and Jane discovered that in the world of business if she worked hard she wasn't treated like a schoolgirl.

Paul noticed both his secretary's looks and her brains, and after using her in a series of promotional posters as 'The Lassiters Girl', he started grooming her for promotion. Jane began to wear sharper suits and take tougher decisions and was soon climbing the ladder of success.

Things went well for Jane in Ramsay Street until she came between her best friend and her husband. When Scott Robinson asked her for help with resitting his HSC she was only too willing to coach her friend through his exams. But as the two spent more and more time together it became clear they would not be able to deny the attraction between them, and eventually they kissed. Their embrace was spotted and soon Charlene had thrown Scott out and was refusing to speak to Jane. Jane had long since split up with Mike – although at one point it looked like they might follow Scott and Charlene down the aisle – but she still had no interest in Scott. It was several weeks before she was able to barge in on Charlene and set her straight. Even though Scott and Charlene got back together, Jane wasn't forgiven until she was injured when she fell from Mike's motorbike and Charlene realized that Jane was her best friend after all.

Once Jane had split from Mike, it seemed the scriptwriters were unsure what sort of man she'd go for. At one point they had her engaged to a wealthy American she had met on a business trip in the States, and she was inexplicably flaunting herself in front of dowdy Des Clarke!

Her gran, on the other hand, had found a man who wanted to marry her. John Worthington was an English gentleman who had plenty of regard for Nell's high-minded ways. His attention even softened the old witch and so he was popular with the neighbours, especially when they learned that he planned to marry Nell and take her away from Ramsay Street to the other side of the world; to Britain.

At one time it had looked like Mrs Mangel was going to ensnare Harold

JOE MANGEL

Mark Little

Joe was absolutely nothing like his mother, Mrs Mangel. He was an unreconstructed oaf who liked his beer, his betting and the status quo. He arrived in Erinsborough shortly before his mum married John Worthington, and when he realized he'd have a roof over his head and there were plenty of gardens that needed his green fingers, he decided to put down some roots of his own. He already had one failed marriage behind him (which had given him his son Toby), when he fell for neighbour Kerry Bishop. It was a case of opposites attracting and, after considerable badgering, he got her to accept his marriage proposal. But just after Kerry had discovered she was pregnant she was killed in a shooting accident. His lodger, Melanie Pearson, helped him through his grief and the custody battle for Kerry's daughter, Sky, and in time they too fell for each other and Melanie became his third wife. They left for a honeymoon in England.

Bishop, who lodged with her when his Christian sensibilities couldn't allow him to live with Madge until their marriage. Stealing Madge's man would have been a sweet success for the shrew-like Nell as the two women were sworn enemies and competed viciously at every level – be it for a job or at a cake baking competition. Apart from Harold, Jane and John, the only other 'person' to see Mrs Mangel's good points was Bouncer the dog. In a stand-off, he chose her over his original owner, Mike, and Mrs Mangel was devoted to the dog who she spoilt rotten.

Shortly before Nell and John's wedding, her brutish son Joe put in an appearance, probably hoping to discover that his step-dad-to-be was loaded, knowing Joe. Even though John was just a modest man of modest means, there was still a benefit to Joe in moving to Erinsborough – it got him away from his nagging wife Noeline.

After his mum's wedding and departure for a new life in Britain, Joe made his mark on number 32, much to his niece Jane's annoyance. The only thing the two shared were a couple of genes, and Joe's choice of entertainment – the footie and a couple of tinnies (or more) – clashed with Jane's desire for some light music and a good book. She felt even more unwelcome in her own home after Noeline (who Joe

had now divorced) arrived on the doorstep with a present for her ex – their eight-year-old son Toby.

Joe initially viewed having his son around as a chore and it was left to Jane to see that her young cousin was fed and taken to school. But Toby was growing up into an intelligent young boy (he'd obviously got his brains from Jane's side of the family) and Joe soon realized that he was proud of his son. So Joe was more than happy to take full-time care of Tobes, as he called him, when Noeline died.

Jane soon left to join her gran in St Albans, where she'd settled, but Joe didn't have to take care of Toby by himself for long because love was about to walk into his life in the shape of Harold Bishop's hippie daughter, Kerry.

On the face of it, Kerry and Joe were another of Ramsay Street's famously mis-matched couples, but it was just a classic case of opposites attracting. Kerry was considerate where Joe was blunt, thoughtful when Joe was selfish, and while he loved her unconditionally, she shared her love out to various campaigns and causes. Kerry was Ramsay Street's very own greenie who separated and recycled her rubbish, persuaded Joe not to use his car, made her family eat organic vegetables and played the role of everyone else's conscience. The thing they did have in common, though, was their status as single parents – Kerry had given birth to her baby daughter Sky while backpacking round the world.

When Joe proposed marriage Kerry turned him down, not because she didn't love him but because she viewed the institution of marriage as outdated and patriarchal. She was willing to compromise, however, so she moved into number 32 with Sky. Nell would have been horrified that her son was cohabiting out of wedlock, but even she found it hard to meddle from 13,000 miles away and the Mangel-Bishops were a strong enough family unit not to need a marriage certificate.

Nevertheless, Joe still wanted Kerry to be his wife and for the children's sake he wanted things to be official. After much pestering (from both Joe and her father Harold), Kerry eventually agreed to tie the knot and they exchanged vows in a beautiful ceremony in a butterfly house.

Sadly, their marriage was to be a short one. Just as Kerry had learned to put her family before her causes, one of her travel buddies who was a real environmental activist turned up and re-ignited Kerry's passion for animal rights. She persuaded Kerry to participate in a protest against poachers, and as Joe couldn't persuade her not to, he went with her on the protest to protect her because she was pregnant. But he could do nothing to save his bride when she was hit by a stray poacher's bullet – all he could do was cradle her in his arms as she died.

As Joe wasn't Sky's natural father there was some doubt as to whether he would be able to obtain custody of the girl, especially since her father Eric – once an idle hippie – was now a respectable suit-wearing businessman. Joe, in his overalls, didn't stand a chance, despite his, Harold's and Toby's testimonies to the authorities, and Sky went to live with her natural father.

On his regular visits, Joe realized that Sky was unhappy with Eric and that he and his wife didn't give her the attention she had received at number 32. Unable to face a new custody battle, Joe took things into his own hands and snatched the child. It was the worst thing he could have done – no court was ever going to give custody of a young child to someone with a criminal record for kidnapping. Sky was returned to Eric, and Joe and Toby mourned their loss. It wasn't long, however, before Eric realized he couldn't cope with looking after his daughter and brought her back to number 32 where he knew she would be better taken care of, especially now that there was another woman in Joe's life.

Joe's relationship with new lodger Melanie Pearson was strictly platonic, but she was still willing to do more than her fair share of baby-sitting and helping with homework, since she had come to love the two children as if they were her own. Meanwhile, Joe had come to love Melanie, but just as he found the courage to tell her how he felt, she started dating another man. Scatty as Melanie was, she could still see that Joe was lonely and looking for love, and so out of friendship she arranged for him to be a contestant on the TV dating show 'Dream Date'. And when one of the contestants dropped out, she stepped into the breach and disguised her voice so Joe would not know it was her.

Of course, they were made for each other and it was a foregone conclusion that Joe would pick Melanie no matter how she spoke, and their prize was a romantic weekend away. Joe was overjoyed at his choice of guest and could contain his ardour no longer. He phoned her hotel room from his and asked to meet. The penny dropped and Melanie realized she felt the same way; when they met in the hotel corridor they couldn't keep their hands off each other!

And it wasn't just Joe who was happy: Toby, Sky and the rest of Ramsay Street were chuffed that these two had got it together after everyone else had known they were perfect for each other for months! A wedding was hastily arranged, and while Joe and Melanie went on honeymoon to England to see Nell, taking Sky with them, Toby went to stay with Dorothy Burke next door. They had such a good time in England, and John's contacts meant they could easily be set up with work and accommodation, that they decided to stay, leaving Toby on a semipermanent basis with Dorothy.

Number 32 then went up for auction and on the day of the sale all the Ramsay Street residents came out to see who their new neighbour was going to be. When the bidding stopped the woman who still had her hand in the air was Rosemary Daniels – no one thought that such a high flyer would want a suburban house when she could have a New York penthouse, and the mystery was explained when she revealed she was acting for her mother. Helen didn't want to live in the house, she simply saw it as an investment and rented it out for a while to Doug Willis's gregarious sister Faye and her son Cameron.

When Julie returned to Erinsborough with her brood, Helen let her granddaughter and family live there as there was a separate room for Hannah, Debbie and Michael, if he chose to return home. Moving to number 32 was a chance for the Martins to start again. Philip had got a job at Lassiters and both the girls were doing well at school – even if Debbie was seeing more of Rick Alessi than her parents would have liked. If ever there was going to be a time they could cope with having

Michael around it was now. Julie was even prepared to decorate and furnish his room herself in an attempt to build bridges with her recalcitrant stepson – and also to prove to Philip that she would do anything for his family.

But her good intentions only caused grief. Hannah, and especially Debbie,

felt Michael was getting preferential treatment and being rewarded for going to the detention centre – and when Michael did come home he thought the only reason Julie had put a TV in his room was so that he wouldn't watch it with them!

Julie and Michael were an even match for each other and equally capable of scheming and being spiteful – and Julie didn't even have the excuse of being a teenager, so it was no wonder Michael hated her so much ... But no one ever thought he would try to kill her. Michael was willing to take his time as he didn't want a murder conviction for doing away with the nastiest piece of work Ramsay

Street had seen since Mrs Mangel left. His plan was to make Julie think she was going crazy: he made telephone calls to her and then denied that he had; he moved things around in the house; he told Julie she'd said things when she hadn't; and, after many months, his plan started working. Julie became convinced she was losing her mind and went to the doctor for medication.

Things were going exactly to Michael's plan – now all he had to do was make Julie take an overdose. He spiked her food and her drinks, changed her dosage without her knowing, and gradually the build-up of poison started to kill her. It was only when she saw a video of Phoebe and Stephen's wedding in which Michael was captured spiking her drink on film that she was able to prove his menace. The boy was punished and banished, but was soon to return.

When he knocked on the door of number 32 he was clutching his side and claimed to be very ill. Julie told him she'd had enough of his sick tricks and that he wasn't welcome. But when Philip arrived home from Lassiters he found his only son unconscious on the porch – he had been ill after all. After rushing Michael to hospital, Philip took out his anger on Julie; Michael could have died because of her.

This was the first crack in a crumbling marriage. Julie had always been difficult to live with, but since finding out that Jim wasn't her real father her personality had undergone a sea-change. Philip didn't think he could take it any more and moved into a suite at Lassiters. Debbie and Hannah stayed on at number 32 with their mother. They even got to the stage of calling in the lawyers after Philip had a brief (and unconsummated) affair with Beth Brennan. Julie had the car yard to support her and the

MELANIE PEARSON
Lucinda Cowden

Mad Mel made her first appearance in Ramsay Street on the arm of Henry Ramsay when her foghorn laugh made Madge pray that Henry wasn't serious about her. She made such an impression that the producers brought her back as Paul's temporary secretary where she was such a hit she was given a permanent role. Melanie was given to wearing outrageous clothes, putting her foot in it and getting in a muddle about most things. After being a bridesmaid at Paul and Chrissie's wedding she somehow managed to end up sleeping in the honeymoon suite on their cruise ship! But she had a heart of gold and thought nothing of putting herself out for others. She did have a hard time with men. After Henry she became engaged to an older man, until she realized she was the same age as his daughter. She dated Simon Hunter who later tried to rape Gaby Willis, and was oblivious to the fact that she was living with her perfect mate, Joe Mangel, who she married in 1994.

girls and if Philip wanted to leave her then she would show him that she didn't need him. She was far too busy trying to track down her real father anyway.

Julie's true paternity had been uncovered when Helen had read some of the letters

PHILIP MARTIN

Ian Rawlings

When Philip first appeared in *Neighbours* it was as the new manager of the local branch of the Pacific Bank, where he was seen as a sleazy married man taking advantage of one of his young tellers, Julie Robinson. But as time progressed we learned his wife was an alcoholic and that he really did love Julie. So when his first wife killed herself and seriously injured him while drunk at the wheel, it seemed right that Julie should go to look after him and his two children, Michael and Debbie. They later had a child of their own, Hannah, and returned to Erinsborough in 1993 (Philip having recovered from his injuries!), where he became the manager of Lassiters. Philip is a placid, easy-going guy who loves his family and the quiet life – so much so that he jacked in his job at Lassiters to run a newsagency as a family business. After Julie's death in 1995, he was shocked when younger medical student Jen Handley took a fancy to him, but when Hannah told him to go for it, he asked Jen to move in with him.

Jim had sent to her daughter, Anne, while she was packing up his things after his death. It became clear that Jim had always known that his elder daughter's real father was a man called Roger Bannon from Queensland. The curiosity about the mysterious Roger Bannon proved too much for Julie and she tried to track him down. She eventually located his widow who told her the worst thing she had ever heard in her life: she was the product of a rape.

This knowledge affected Julie deeply and her behaviour became even more insufferable, bringing divorce a step closer. But in their war, Philip and Julie had over-looked the most injured casualty – Hannah. Still not yet ten years old, Hannah took her parents' split hard, and it was Debbie who noticed her little sister had started wetting her bed.

Hannah's misery was enough for Philip to think twice about the split, and he returned to Ramsay Street to give his marriage another go. Julie took the opportunity to tell him about her father and the shame she felt, but Philip reassured her he was more interested in the future than the past.

The Martins rejoiced and resolved to work hard at their marriage, and so when

Philip realized that not only did his job at Lassiters take him away from his family but also made him tired and stressed when he was with them, he decided to jack the job in. Only he didn't tell Julie first and when she found out she hit the roof: how dare he give up their financial security without discussing it with her? When Philip told her that he had bought the local newsagency to run as a family business this was the final straw. The rows started again, and their relationship went from bad to worse. This time it was Debbie who was to pay the price. She stopped eating, altogether it seemed, until Cody discovered a secret store of chocolate and buns in her bedroom and instantly diagnosed her friend as bulimic.

Friends and family rallied round the stricken teen and it looked like their support was all she needed as Debbie started eating meals with her family again. But Debbie had just found better ways of hiding her bingeing. It soon became clear that she needed professional help and she was booked into a residential clinic. Even though Debbie's illness had given Philip and Julie a reason to unite, it was clear their marriage was in a downward spiral and the rows and name-calling got worse.

When Debbie was in the clear, Philip decided he needed a holiday from his wife and his marriage and joined some of the neighbours on a murder mystery weekend. Julie, clearly recognizing that her marriage was in need of emergency surgery, followed Philip to the hotel where he was staying to make a last-ditch attempt to save their union. But before she could make him hear sense she got exceedingly drunk and had an accident. At first some thought it was all part of the murder mystery plot, but it became clear Julie's injuries were serious and she was rushed to hospital where the family, including Michael, prayed for her recovery. Michael told her he was sorry for all the things he'd done and Philip realized how trivial their problems were in the face of her accident.

But nothing they said or anything the doctors did could save her. Julie's funeral was going to be a hard day for all the family, but it was made worse when Philip was arrested at the graveside for his wife's murder. Certainly there were many witnesses who could testify to hearing Philip curse his wife of late, but no one really thought he could have done it. He was still the number-one suspect, however, even though several other people had said even worse things about her in the past. It wasn't until Debbie had a flashback to the fateful night that the circumstances of Julie's death were revealed; they had been so traumatic Debbie had blocked them out. Julie had got so drunk that she had simply fallen from the top of a building, and once the circumstantial evidence bore this story out, Philip was released.

Julie's death not only affected Philip deeply (he started drinking heavily) but it also took its toll on Helen, and the Martins had moved back into number 26 to be with her. Number 32 was empty for a while, but not for long.

Helen decided to sell the house and it was bought by Philip Martin. He rented it out to teen lovers Mal Kennedy and Danni Stark so they could have some privacy away from their interfering parents across the street. The house then became home to Stonefish, a school friend of Cody and Danni's, and his mother Angie.

BABY *Neighbours*

There's a very famous saying that actors should never work with children or animals, but *Neighbours'* stars have always had to work with both. Apart from a constant string of pets – Bouncer, Oscar the snake, Rosie, Holly – there have also been a number of scene-stealing babies in Ramsay Street.

James Kingsley Clarke was the first baby to be born in *Neighbours*, and, like most births in soap, he didn't arrive when he was expected. He chose to say his first hello to his parents, Des and Daphne, while they were enjoying a picnic. And Jamie continued to be something of a trouble-maker, both on and off screen. In the two years he lived on Ramsay Street he was played by three different actors – one of whom was a girl! On screen, Jamie was passed from Mrs Kirkwood the childminder to dad Des and finally nanny Bronwyn after his mum Daphne died.

The next baby to find himself in Ramsay Street was Sam Cole. Madge got the shock of her life one evening when she came home to find a sixteen-year-old Charlene cradling a baby – and claiming it was hers. Although Charlene made up a story convincing enough for Madge to believe she was a grandmother, Sam wasn't Charlene's son; he was her half-brother. Sam had been born to Susan Cole after Madge's ex-husband Fred had had an affair with her, and when Fred had turned nasty, Susan turned to Charlene for support. Susan had no way of looking after Sam without Fred's help and Charlene knew it. She also knew that Madge wouldn't be happy looking after the 'other woman's' baby, so she claimed Sam was hers.

Madge eventually uncovered the truth, but instead of being mad at Charlene and Susan she was actually relieved to discover that it wasn't just her Fred had treated badly, but every woman he became involved with. Susan and Sam stayed at number 24 for a while before moving in with Clive Gibbons at number 22. Clive fell for Susan and was a natural with Sam, but Susan had fallen for Paul. When Paul rejected her advances, Susan shot through, taking Sam with her.

Jim's second wife Beverly thought she was a career woman who didn't want any children, but her biological clock was ticking and a hormonal alarm-bell went off. Although Jim was not keen to have more children, he could appreciate that his wife was desperate for a baby, and he agreed to start trying. When Beverly fell pregnant but then miscarried, they applied to adopt but were turned down because Jim was too old. Beverly was allowed to foster, however, and she was given baby Rhys to care for. She was an obsessive mother, never letting Rhys out of her arms or her sight. And so when he was taken back by his natural parents, Beverly's world fell apart and it signalled the end of an already strained marriage.

There have been surprisingly few births – only five – in *Neighbours'* ten-year history. Perhaps this is because a pregnancy storyline needs nine months and most characters don't seem to hang around long enough! It was four long years after Jamie's birth that the next maternity-ward scenes had to be scripted – and they were for Christina Alessi as she proudly showed the world her and Paul's son, Andrew, for the first time.

When Christina went into labour she was out shopping, and as the baby was coming so fast there was no time to call Paul and let him know.

But she didn't need to because Paul was at home at the time, as was Chrissie's twin sister Caroline. And when Caroline inexplicably doubled up with a searing pain in her abdomen, she knew Chrissie had gone into labour. Paul didn't dismiss Caroline's pain because she had also shared sympathetic food cravings and morning sickness when Chrissie was in the early stages of the pregnancy. And so dad and aunt dashed to the hospital and arrived just in time to help Chrissie through the final stages.

DAPHNE CLARKE
Elaine Smith

After ten years, Daphne is still one of the most popular people to have lived in Ramsay Street. Her no-nonsense approach to most situations and her lack of apologies for making her living as a stripper immediately endeared her to the viewers. Her spiky hair and bright clothes made her stand out from other women on TV, and her ability to treat teenagers as adults was a winner with younger viewers. As the owner of the Coffee Shop, Daff was privy to much of the teenage angst that flooded Erinsborough and often mediated between kids and their parents – most notably when she took abused teen Mike Young under her wing. She never had any problems dating men – Shane Ramsay, Clive Gibbons and Paul Robinson were all queuing up – but Daff shocked her friends by marrying boring Des Clarke and settling down to suburban life and motherhood. She was injured in a car crash on the way to her dad's funeral in 1989 and rushed to hospital where she lay in a coma for almost a month before the scriptwriters finally let go of the street's most colourful neighbour.

(Incidentally, of all the babies used in *Neighbours* the baby used to play Andrew was considered the best behaved. Even when they wanted him to cry he wouldn't!)

Phoebe Bright was the next woman to become pregnant in Ramsay Street, and her imminent motherhood came as something of a shock. Despite deciding to have an abortion, Todd's death on the way to the clinic to prevent the operation going ahead convinced Phoebe that she should have the child, even though she knew being a single, teenage mum would be hard. As it happened, she found she wouldn't have to go

through motherhood alone as she met and fell in love with Stephen Gottlieb, who she married.

The only other babies to be logged on the Ramsay Street registrar's books were born on the same day in the same hospital. When Gaby Willis returned home after several months away to inform her parents that she was pregnant, mature mum Cheryl Stark also announced she was with child. But as Gaby was two months further on in her pregnancy, everyone expected the younger woman to go into labour first.

In true *Neighbours* style though, things didn't go as planned. So while Gaby was giving birth to a healthy baby boy in one ward, Cheryl was rushed to another ward to have her daughter prematurely. Both Gaby and son were doing well, but it was an anxious time for Lou as both his daughter and his partner fought for their lives. In just a matter of episodes, however, Cheryl and the new arrival were in the clear – now the biggest problem for the couple was naming their child.

Lou and Cheryl had to fight over not just first names but the surname for their baby daughter. Since they weren't married, both of them wanted the child to have their surname. In the end a compromise was reached and the girl was named Louise Stark, although she is affectionately known as Lolly.

PHOEBE BRIGHT

Simone Robertson

When Phoebe first appeared in *Neighbours* it was as a figure of fun. The school swot, she was called 'Creepy Phoebe' because of her passion for keeping pet reptiles, her favourite of which was Oscar the snake. But both Josh and then Todd fell for her and she blossomed. The product of a broken home, Dorothy Burke took Phoebe in after her father died, and despite Dorothy's careful watch, Phoebe still managed to get pregnant by Todd Landers. Phoebe expected Mrs Burke – or Mim as she called her – to blow a fuse when she told her about the baby, but instead Dorothy was supportive and even went to the abortion clinic with her. Phoebe kept the

baby, of course, and when Stephen Gottlieb approached her at Todd's graveside he was as attracted to the idea of a ready-made family as he was to Phoebe. She agreed to marry Stephen even though she didn't love him – although she soon learned to – and by the time Stephen was offered his dream job of working in a record store in Anson's Corner, Phoebe was more than happy to follow her husband anywhere in the world.

BAD *Neighbours*

Every good story has a good baddie. Villains are as much a part of soaps – and any other form of storytelling – as heroes and cliffhangers, and *Neighbours* has certainly had its fair share. But as *Neighbours* is by nature an easy-going soap with upbeat storylines and likeable characters, the baddies that have entered Ramsay Street have usually gone as quickly as they came. With a few notable exceptions, of course.

Without a doubt, the nastiest person in *Neighbours'* history was Paul Robinson. His list of crimes is longer than the telephone directory, and the only reason he got away with so much was because he was a charmer too. But he wasn't always a bad boy; in fact, in the early days he was really quite nice! Jim always expected his studious older son to follow him into engineering, but Paul's marriage to crook's moll Terri Inglis changed all that. When she shot him to prevent him reporting her to the police for murder, she killed off the warmer parts of his character. Hurt and angry, Paul became bitter, selfish and determined – qualities his aunt Rosemary realized would make him a ruthless businessman and so she gave him the job of running the Daniels Corporation in Australia.

There wasn't a single trick Paul wouldn't use to get his own way: when a supermarket development needed to demolish local housing to build an access road he set to work using his 'contacts' to evict his family and neighbours from Ramsay Street.

Paul's charm meant he never had a hard time attracting women, but he never failed to treat them badly. Even when his second wife Gail was heavily pregnant he wouldn't tear himself away from work to be with her. She used to say that he 'worshipped the almighty dollar' and she was right. If there was a buck to be made, Paul didn't care if he had to stab a friend in the back to get it. Gail left him, but he easily replaced her with his third wife, Christina, whose loyalty and love he repaid with adultery. And to prove what a nasty man he was, he didn't just cheat on her with any woman – he chose her twin sister. Although he managed to repair his marriage and start again with Chrissie in Hawaii, Paul returned to Ramsay Street to show his family once and for all what a thoroughly rotten egg he was. In a desperate bid for cash he tried to embezzle funds from Lassiters and Philip Martin's private company, and was willing to let his brother-in-law go to prison for his crime.

But as Paul caught a taxi to the airport and a life on the run in Brazil, his conscience was pricked and he handed the driver a letter to take to the police which exonerated Philip. So disgusted were his family by his behaviour that he

PAUL ROBINSON

Stefan Dennis

One of the soap's most enduring characters, Paul stayed in Ramsay Street for seven-and-a-half years. In that time he married three times and fathered five children: Amy, by a colleague from the airline he worked with for a while; the triplets by wife number two Gail Lewis; and Andrew by his third wife, Christina. A central figure not just because of his family connections but also because of the power he wielded around the Lassiters complex, Paul was never far removed from the action. Despite his overpowering traits as a control freak and money-making machine, Paul was capable of moments of kindness, especially in regard to his gran, Helen. He was very good at recognizing talent in other people and often took a chance on a less qualified person if he thought they had the nous and ambition to cut it. He currently lives in Rio de Janeiro with Chrissie and Andrew, where he is avoiding arrest for fraud.

hasn't had the guts to set foot in Erinsborough since.

One of the other few long-term baddies in *Neighbours* was Mrs Mangel. It is just possible that Nell Mangel may have been a nicer person when she was younger, but by the time she lived in Ramsay Street she was as bitter as a lemon and as twisted as old rope. In fact her only source of fun seemed to be found in other people's misery. She never committed a crime (although some suspected she had done away with her husband Len at one point), but she was in constant contact with the police. She reported everything that happened in the street, even things as petty as dropping litter. She was as feared by her neighbours as a real crook for her knack of turning someone else's misfortune into a matter for the law.

Most of *Neighbours'* baddies have been transient; the forces of good overpower them and send them on to their next victim – or prison. In the early days crime boss Charles Durham involved Terri Inglis in his murderous plots, conman Douglas Blake tricked Helen out of her life savings and, over the years, they have been replaced by a string of mean-minded no-gooders. Annalise Hartman was sexually harassed by her boss, Jeffrey Hockney, when she took an office job; a client of Lassiters called Simon Hunter tried to rape Gaby Willis, and Annalise's mum, Fiona, tried to con Jim Robinson out of his money – and succeeded. But none of these characters hung around for long. The next baddies to stay put, perhaps unsurprisingly, were relatives of Paul's.

His sister Julie wasn't evil like her brother, but she was so insensitive and selfish that she was hated just the same. However, it was her stepson Michael Martin who proved to be the real baddie in the family.

Michael hadn't always been a rotter and his bad behaviour only started when his dad began his relationship with Julie. Michael blamed Julie for his mum's death and never accepted her as a stepmother. He took pleasure in making her life hell. He was always in and out of the juvenile detention centre for crimes ranging from robbery to violent behaviour, but his worst crime by far was trying to kill Julie. Even when Michael's plan to poison her was uncovered, Philip was still unwilling to write off his only son and, after he hadn't heard from him in several months, he hired a detective to find him. In the end though it was Rick Alessi who found Michael by bumping into him on Bondi Beach while taking a break in Sydney. Julie, naturally, wasn't pleased to have her stepson around again, but he was soon in trouble once more and found himself back in the detention centre. While he was inside he made an enemy of Darren Stark (Cheryl's elder son) who vowed to get Michael when he was released. But Darren wasn't intending to get to Michael by beating him up, he was planning something far worse than that – he was going to hurt Debbie.

When Darren was released he kept his promise and made his way to Ramsay Street where he assumed another name and set about wooing Debbie so he could lure her into one of his dangerous schemes. He succeeded, and planned to involve her in a dangerous petrol station hold-up. Through his contacts Michael found out about this and asked Rick to help him escape. Rick's hare-brained scheme involved dressing Michael in clothes he'd stolen from Helen Daniels' washing line, but it worked. Michael was embarrassed but determined to show his father that he'd do anything for the people he loved and rushed to the petrol station just in time to catch a bullet that was heading straight for his little sister. This selfless deed did much to restore him in the eyes of the neighbours, but everyone had learned to trust Michael at their peril.

MICHAEL MARTIN

Troy Beckwith

Michael was proof that girls prefer bad boys, as he never had any problems attracting women. When he dated Danni Stark their parents disapproved of such a serious relationship in a couple so young, but their efforts to keep them apart only made the two try harder to sneak out and see each other. In one of *Neighbours'* more educational storylines, Danni and Michael discussed sleeping together, but in their lust forgot to use contraception. A pregnancy scare taught them – and many of the teenage viewers – a big lesson. Michael also dated Cody Willis, but before they slept together Michael discovered an ex-girlfriend had tested positive for HIV and was now living rough. Michael later tested negative. Philip pushed his son to get some educational qualifications but Helen suggested an outback hostel for young offenders where he would receive tuition in carpentry and other practical skills. Michael agreed to give it his best shot and by all accounts is finally on the straight and narrow.

GOOD-LOOKING *Neighbours*

Neighbours was originally bought by the BBC because they thought the location scenes filmed in the Australian sunshine would be a way of brightening up their schedules in the gloomy British climate. But of course the real switch-on factor wasn't the sun or the quickly-realized plots, it was the endless stream of good-looking guys and gorgeous girls. And the hot Aussie sunshine always provided them with the perfect excuse for the boys to take their shirts off and for the girls to sunbathe in as little as possible!

The 'easy-on-the-eye' factor was exploited right from the beginning when Shane was often seen down at the diving pool in nothing but a pair of Speedos and sporting an equally impressive pair of biceps. The producers soon became aware of how big a draw the poolside scenes were – especially with viewers in dreary Britain – and so when Shane's diving career was cut short in a car crash, Max Ramsay started training Mike Young, who looked even better in a pair of skimpy shorts! But the biggest sex symbol in the early days was undoubtedly Scott Robinson. After the character had been recast with Jason Donovan and the great romance had started with Charlene, Scott became every girl's dream date (a few mothers wouldn't have minded either!). His blond hair, lean body and bronzed skin was a hit and soon it seemed every episode had a scene at the beach where either Scott and Charlene or Mike and Jane would have to cool their passions with a swim. Once, when Scott and Charlene were at the beach with Mike and Helen's niece Nikki, the girls persuaded the boys to go skinny dipping. But when Mike and Scott got naked and ran into the water, the girls ran off with their clothes, leaving the boys to cover their modesty as best they could while they walked to a phone box to get a lift home.

The next actor to endure the embarrassment of a nude scene was Charlene's brother Henry, who became a surprise favourite with the teen magazines when his big muscles and sense of fun won over the audience. In fact, *Neighbours* has produced several unlikely sex symbols including Clive Gibbons, Brett Stark, Michael Martin and Joe Mangel, whose personalities have triumphed over their ordinary looks to claim the viewers' affections.

Henry had to bare all when the door slammed shut behind him, trapping the corner of the towel which was the only thing he was wearing after having a shower. Stranded outside, he was forced to make a quick streak to let himself back in. It might have been a tricky moment for Henry, but it was certainly a favourite one for his fans!

SCOTT ROBINSON

Jason Donovan

The youngest of Jim Robinson's sons didn't gel with the viewers until he was recast with Jason Donovan when the show was picked up by Channel Ten. He became the show's pin-up as he dated and married Charlene, failed his HSC, skateboarded around town and tried hard to be a man before his time. Although he was only with the show for three years, the character left his mark on Ramsay Street and set the standard the casting directors had to meet every time a young stud came into the show. Scott's ambition was to be a journalist, but for a long time the closest he got to working for a newspaper was delivering it. He then got a cadetship on the *Erinsborough News*,

where he got into trouble reporting on his neighbours' private business. When Charlene moved to Brisbane Scott stayed behind until he could get another cadetship on a Brisbane paper, which eventually came through. Scott and Charlene have defied the odds; they are still together and have a son, Daniel.

Once *Neighbours'* reputation for having the hottest bodies on television had been established, the producers started casting even more beautiful people and occasionally used models instead of actors to keep viewers glued. Both actresses who played Annalise Hartman and Gaby Willis were former models who got their acting breaks on *Neighbours*. But while the show has been careful not to alienate its audience by having too many beautiful people, it has always made sure that when one hunk left, he was quickly replaced by another.

After Scott and Mike came Josh (whose body was shown off with flair when he became a stripagram), Jim's nephew Matt and recalcitrant artist Nick Page. Then there was Lou's brooding son Guy, Pam and Doug Willis's eldest, Adam, and their nephew, Cameron. Of course, there have also been plenty of beautiful girls living in the street: Jane and Charlene were replaced by Bronwyn and Gemma; then the twins moved in, as did Gaby, Annalise and Beth. And there have been enough beauty contests, aspiring models and sporting storylines to ensure that it wasn't just their faces the viewers got a good look at!

It didn't take much brain power to guess that beautiful Caroline and Christina Alessi came from good-looking stock, but when their cousins Marco and Rick arrived in Ramsay Street the viewers went wild for their hunky Italian looks. Rick, played by Dan Falzon, became one of the most photographed stars of the show. But he certainly had some stiff competition in the hunk stakes. Just three doors down there was Brad Willis, whose surfer's physique and shoulder-length blond hair attracted a lot of attention. When Brad left, the scriptwriters introduced another good-looking guy to the show in the form of Sam Kratz, just to make sure the viewers were still paying attention.

Naturally it made sense to pair the good-looking characters off into hot couples, so there was always someone delectable on screen for everyone to swoon over! And so Gaby Willis found herself dating Jim's son Glen Donnelly, followed by the object of many schoolgirl crushes – teacher Wayne Duncan, before getting pregnant by rugged Jack Flynn and seeing dashing Kris, her personal assistant at Lassiters, before leaving the show. Annalise Hartman's love life was equally filled with handsome fellas (if you don't include Lou, of course!) and when Mark was finished with her, she found herself in the arms of Sam Kratz and – briefly – Stonefish's too. More recently, Danni Stark has been paired off with Michael, Rick and finally Mal Kennedy. Of course it hasn't been just the women who've been passed from hunk to hunk: Brad found himself pursued by Lucy and Lauren before settling down with Beth.

As well as attracting the viewers, *Neighbours'* gorgeous guys and beautiful babes have also attracted the individual actors a lot of attention from the press – and not all of it has been wanted. Many have had to employ personal managers and agents, not just to co-ordinate their busy schedules but also to protect them from the more unsavoury aspects of being in the public eye. In the early days, around the time of Scott and Charlene's wedding, Kylie Minogue and Jason Donovan were mobbed by fans. Tens of thousands of people turned up in shopping centres and the like as they promoted the show. Later though, when the newspapers had cottoned on to the fact that stories about these teen sensations would boost their circulation, cameras followed them wherever they went, and pictures of Kylie sunbathing topless in Bali were printed all over the world.

This sort of attention has made the *Neighbours'* boys and babes stars wherever they go, something that theatre promoters in the UK exploit every Christmas when it seems half the cast arrive in the country for the panto season!

RICK ALESSI

Dan Falzon

Benito Alessi had hoped of great things from his younger son, but when Rick turned his back on a private education for a summer of fun with his elder brother, Marco, Benito knew he had to take Rick in hand. But Rick was always able to get round his dad – he even managed to go to London without Ben noticing! He lost his virginity to long-time girlfriend Debbie Martin, and when they split up had a promiscuous period which ended when he fell for an older woman, Sally, who dented his pride by refusing him. He later fell in love with Cody Willis but left her when his career in hotel management led him to a course in America. He returned to Ramsay Street but then left to go and work for Gaby Willis in Darwin. Rick's zany nature and love of good times, however, didn't exactly make him an obvious choice for responsibility.

MORTAL

Neighbours

Killing off a character in a soap is never an easy decision. While it is a sure-fire way of boosting the ratings, producers don't want to kill off popular characters in case they ever want to bring them back. Sometimes, though, when an actor is sure that he or she will never return then it's a chance for a really gripping storyline that producers seize with both hands.

Saying a permanent farewell to a minor character is less problematic, as it can often bring about major plot changes: lead characters can be accused of murder, have a reason to leave town, or arrive in Ramsay Street unexpectedly. And so over the years Shane's been accused of murder when his car crashed and killed someone, Danni and Rick were wracked with guilt when a car prank went wrong, Pam Willis got arrested for

euthanasia when an elderly patient died and Glen Donnelly turned up on Jim's front door when he couldn't pay for his mother's funeral expenses. Sad as it may seem, death makes good drama, and *Neighbours* is at its most dramatic when a major character meets his or her maker.

The first of the regulars to join the big soap opera in the sky was Daphne Clarke, but even the events on screen couldn't match the drama going on behind the cameras. Actress Elaine Smith was keen to leave *Neighbours* after two-and-a-half years on the show, but as Daphne was one of the most popular characters the producers decided not to kill her off. Instead she moved to another part of the city to care for her dying father. But the fans weren't satisfied with this and so Elaine came back to finish off the character – literally. On the way to her father's funeral, Daphne's car crashed leaving her unconscious. She was rushed to hospital where she remained in a coma while the producers tried to persuade Elaine to stay. But she was adamant, and in the end Daphne finally slipped away in July 1989.

It was two years before the decision was taken to kill off another major character and this time it was to be Kerry Bishop. The producers had months to plan Kerry's demise and they decided to make it as poignant as possible. Their first step

was to make the newlywed pregnant, the second was for her stepson Toby to finally accept her into the family and start calling her 'mum'. The final step was to have a greenie friend of Kerry's persuade her to return to her campaigning roots and take part in an anti-poaching demonstration, against her husband Joe's wishes. He soon realized he couldn't stop his wife going on the demo and so vowed to go with her to protect her and their unborn child, so when Kerry was hit by a stray poacher's bullet Joe would be there to cradle his wife and baby. It was a real tearjerker and the producers had manipulated the viewers' emotions to perfection. Kerry's death was also the catalyst for several subsequent storylines, most notably Joe's custody battle for her daughter, Sky. In fact, deaths are such good material for the scriptwriters that it's surprising not more characters are bumped off.

The next fatality in Erinsborough was to be Kerry's dad Harold in 1992. it was supposed to be a happy time for Harold and his wife Madge: they had just come up trumps on the premium bonds and wanted to spend their good fortune on touring Australia. Tragically, they were only a few days from Erinsborough when Harold mysteriously disappeared while walking along some cliffs. Madge only stopped for a minute to talk to a local painter and when she turned round he had gone. She searched frantically for him, as did the coastguard, but it was only when Madge found her husband's glasses in a rock pool that she was forced to conclude that Harold had been washed off the rocks to his death. The sea was searched for his body but it was never recovered.

It is always sad when someone dies, but it is particularly hard to accept when it is a young person – especially one with as much to live for as Todd Landers. Viewers had seen Todd grow up from a geeky kid into a charming young adult, so the producers wanted to say goodbye to him in style and wrote him one of the show's most dramatic exits. While dashing to the clinic to prevent his girlfriend Phoebe from aborting their child, Todd was knocked down by a van. News filtered through to Phoebe that Todd was in casualty, so before she could have the termination she left the clinic and headed for the

TODD LANDERS

Kristian Schmid

Todd arrived in Erinsborough on the day of Scott and Charlene's wedding to be looked after by his aunt, Beverly Marshall, while his parents Bob and Annette went through a rough patch. When his parents' marriage didn't recover, he – and for a while his little sister Katie – stayed on in Ramsay Street. He was a conscientious student but was easily distracted by a string of girlfriends; Melissa Jarrett, Cody Willis (with whom he ran away so they could be together) and Phoebe Bright. He lost his virginity to Phoebe whom he made pregnant and, after much deliberation, the teenagers decided Phoebe should have an abortion. But when Todd, a thoughtful and sensitive lad, changed his mind at the last minute and raced to the abortion clinic, he was knocked down by a van and died later in hospital. Phoebe changed her mind about the abortion and Todd's daughter, Hope, was born in November 1993.

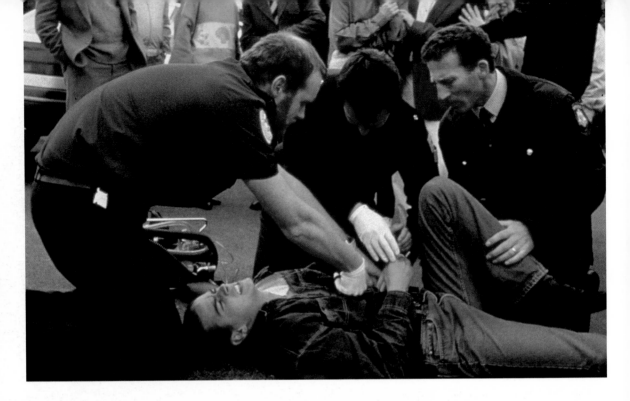

hospital – but arrived only to watch Todd die of a heart attack.

This was not the last we saw of Todd though, this being *Neighbours* he was to return as a ghost to comfort Phoebe through her blackest moments and tell her that the baby she was carrying was a girl. Phoebe doubted what she had seen until she gave birth to a daughter and then accepted that Todd really had been looking out for her.

The next death in Ramsay Street was perhaps the most shocking, because one of the show's two remaining original characters was for the chop. Alan Dale, who played Jim Robinson, had been with *Neighbours* for almost eight years and was pleased when the producers agreed to give one of the most popular characters a send-off to remember. Jim had had a heart scare several years before, but in the intervening years he had taken up cycling in a bid to improve his health. But the stress of starting a relationship with a woman his family despised – schemer Fiona Hartman – raised the pressure and all his exercise had been for nought. After playing with his granddaughter Hannah, Jim

returned home for a lie down as he was feeling weak. But he never made it to his bedroom and suffered a massive and fatal heart attack in the kitchen of number 26. For a man with such a large and (generally) loving family, Jim's dying alone was tremendously poignant.

The most recent main character to be killed off was possibly the most popular choice for gruesome death! Julie Robinson Martin may have had a good heart, but she had a hard time showing it to anyone and was consequently disliked by almost everyone. Fittingly for a death surrounded by mystery, Julie's demise took place on a murder mystery weekend. The police had no end of suspects as virtually everyone Julie had ever met had a motive for doing away with her, but at her funeral they dramatically arrested Philip. He was only exonerated when Debbie had a flashback to the fateful night and remembered seeing her mum fall to her death from the roof of the hotel.

And no doubt with storylines like this to excite and intrigue the viewers, many more *Neighbours* regulars will meet a sticky end!

JULIE MARTIN

Julie Mullins

Julie could never keep her nose out of everyone else's business and her brusque and pompous manner meant that her interference was never appreciated! In the early days of the soap, we learned that Julie had dated Des Clarke before falling for her boss Philip Martin. After Philip was seriously injured she left Erinsborough to take care of him and his kids, with whom she returned to Ramsay Street in 1993. Even though she was now played by a different actress, Julie was as obnoxious and unbearable as ever. One of Julie's specialities was embarrassing her children (however unconsciously) and she mortified Debbie when she returned to Erinsborough High to gain the HSC that had eluded her as a teenager. Julie's temperament was unsuited to almost any sort of work, but strangely she found she had a way with female customers when she inherited her dad's half of the car yard and was able to support herself and her daughters through her many separations from Philip.

FEUDING *Neighbours*

There's nothing like a good feud to entertain the viewers; two arch rivals who will seize any and every opportunity to get one over on the other always makes good drama. Over the years, *Neighbours* has had several petty and short-lived feuds, usually over sporting events like the Ramsay Street Olympics, when the Ramsays and the Robinsons tried to prove they could cycle faster, run further and swim better than each other. But every now and then there have been two characters in the street who just couldn't stand the sight of each other, and the first of these great feuds was between Madge Mitchell and Mrs Mangel.

Madge thought Nell was interfering, nosy and after Harold. Nell thought Madge was pompous, gossipy and beneath her. Of course, they were both right! So whenever there was a chance for the two of them to compete it became like world war three, even if it was just a cake baking competition that Helen was bound to win anyway! It was only when Mrs Mangel left for a new life in England that Madge showed her any kindness by wishing her all the best. Thankfully the two actresses got on extremely well when the cameras stopped rolling and there have rarely been reports of feuds going on backstage on the *Neighbours'* set. In fact, it would seem to be the opposite as the studios have a reputation as a hotbed of romance. Over the years several of the stars have started relationships with each other – even, in one case, making it down the aisle when Henry and Bronwyn's marriage was mirrored in real life by the actors who played them!

Madge was also to feature in *Neighbours'* next ongoing feud after she took an instant dislike to prim and proper Dorothy Burke, the local school principal. These two hated each other so much that they would even walk out of a room if the other came in. And what one of them had, the other made sure she had too. So when Dorothy decided to run for the local council, guess who followed suit. In the course of their civic duties Madge and Dorothy had many dealings with another councillor, Felicity Brent, who seemed to be waging a one-woman battle against Paul Robinson. In the end, though, Paul was able to prove Felicity was corrupt and got her thrown off the council, thus nipping what could have been a particularly vicious feud in the bud. Meanwhile, council duties forced Madge and Dorothy to spend even more time in each other's company. At one civic function they found themselves in the ladies' room together just as the caretaker was locking up, and they were forced to spend the entire night locked in together.

Most of *Neighbours'* feuds have been between women, either because they've been fighting over a man or because they simply couldn't stand each other, but at one time there were two men in the street who couldn't even bear to mention each other's names; Lou Carpenter and Benito Alessi.

The two men couldn't have been more different: Lou liked his beer, Ben rarely drank; Lou had two failed marriages behind him, Ben was still with his childhood sweetheart; Lou liked having a good time, Ben didn't know how to let go. So when Lou was forced to sell fifty per cent of his car lot the last person he expected to go into business with him was Benito. But Ben saw Carpenter's Cars as a goldmine if only it was run properly. Ben moved in on Lou's turf with his time-management charts and accountancy documents and tried to make some space for himself in the mess that was Lou's office.

It was only a matter of minutes before they clashed. Benito couldn't believe that Lou would lie about a car's mileage in order to sell it, or claim that a particular year's model was a rarity and therefore worth more. Benito wanted everything by the book and down the line. Lou let him have his way for a time but when profits plummeted Lou was determined to have things done his way. It was war. The fighting went on so long that some sort of cease-fire had to be negotiated, and the answer was simple: they just painted a line down the middle of the forecourt. To the left of it was Lou's terrain and to the right of it was Benito's, and if a customer wanted to look at cars on both sides then they'd have to deal with both of them. The competition between them meant they both worked hard to outperform each other, but while it was good for the bank balance it was hell on the nerves, so Benito conceded defeat and sold his half to Jim, who to Lou's relief told him he was happy to be a silent partner.

Naturally, with so many people in one street dating each other, there have often been bitter rivalries over love. Lucy had to fight Beth Brennan tooth and nail for Brad's affections, and then Beth had to fight Lauren for the same man's love. But the women who have fought with each other the most in *Neighbours* have been Annalise Hartman and Gaby Willis.

Both young, both beautiful, both foul-mouthed where the other was concerned. Gaby thought Annalise was an airhead who set the cause of feminism back a century and Annalise thought Gaby had too high an opinion of herself. It was a recipe for endless catfights and bitchy quips.

What grated Annalise the most was that Gaby was technically her boss when the blonde worked in The Waterhole and the brunette managed Lassiters. Whenever they appeared on screen together the temperature cooled by a measurable amount, but it wasn't until Lassiters employed a sexy new French chef that the two women fought over a man.

Because Gaby had employed Marcel she figured she had first refusal on him, but Annalise also fancied the new arrival and set about seducing him. Even when they discovered that Marcel was in fact a rather less exotic Australian called Mark, they were still after him. It turned into an absurd competition with the two women making fools of themselves in order to be the first to bed her man. In the end they didn't care about Mark at all – just rubbing the other one's face in it was enough.

It was Annalise who eventually won Mark's affections and the two women called a truce, of sorts. Gaby even offered to take Annalise for a trip up in a plane once she'd gained her pilot's licence. But tragedy struck and Gaby's plane fell from the sky in one of the show's most tense cliff-hangers. Gaby survived the crash virtually unscathed but Annalise hit her head

on impact and was unconscious. Although she made a full recovery, Annalise never quite forgave her rival for putting her life in jeopardy and the feud between them deepened.

Things weren't helped when Gaby became pregnant and Mark began to get broody. He desperately wanted Annalise to have a baby, but when she refused Mark started spending

DOROTHY BURKE

Maggie Dence

Many of the neighbours found Dorothy, the Erinsborough High School principal rather prickly. She had severe looks and sharp features and usually wore black, giving her a witch-like appearance. But in truth Dorothy was just a little eccentric. She was well travelled, could speak many languages and clearly had a past that would shock most of her students. She married, but divorced her husband, Colin, after he was convicted of fraud. Although she never had children of her own, Dorothy took care of a long line of children including her niece and nephew Lochie and Ryan, as well as Toby Mangel and Phoebe Bright. As well as her duties at the school, Dorothy was elected to the council – along with sparring partner Madge Bishop – where she undertook more duties for the borough. Love unexpectedly came her way when school inspector Tom Merrick proved to be her soul mate, and in 1993 he whisked her away from Ramsay Street on the back of his motorbike and, along with Toby, they set up house together in the country. Dorothy later took Toby back to live with Joe and Melanie who had returned from England.

more and more time with his girlfriend's arch rival. When the day came that Gaby waved goodbye to Ramsay Street, in 1995, all the neighbours were sad to see her go. All of them, that is, except Annalise who was glad – ecstatic in fact – finally to see the back of the woman who had made her life as hellish as she possibly could.

TOPICAL *Neighbours*

Neighbours is always entertaining, but it's not all an endless round of romance and petty misunderstandings. As the soap has such a large teenage audience, it is always careful to tackle serious issues responsibly and, over the years, *Neighbours* has educated its viewers on several hard-hitting topics.

One of the themes it has returned to time and again has been teenage sex. Whether it's Brett feeling embarrassed because he's still a virgin or a young couple discussing sleeping together for the first time, *Neighbours* has always explained the facts. The first teen couple to talk about sleeping together were Todd and Cody, but they both decided they were too young and it wasn't until Todd started dating Phoebe that he lost his virginity.

Obviously, if teenagers were depicted having sex quite happily in every episode, then certain people would be up in arms accusing *Neighbours* of encouraging promiscuity among the young. And so no teen has ever made love without the sobering experience of a pregnancy scare, like Danni and Michael, Debbie and Rick or Danni and Mal. But in Phoebe's case it was more than a scare – she *was* pregnant. Together Phoebe and Todd shared their shock with the viewers as they maturely discussed adoption and abortion as two of their options. When they decided to abort the baby, *Neighbours* was keen to show that this hadn't been an easy decision and right up until the last minute Phoebe was hounded by pro-life protesters calling her a murderer. Of course, as we now know, Phoebe kept the baby following Todd's death, but the scriptwriters avoided a single mum storyline by marrying her off to Stephen.

As well as the threat of pregnancy, sexually transmitted diseases have also been subjects of angst among Ramsay Street's teenagers. After sleeping with Brad, Lauren thought she was pregnant even though a pregnancy test showed she wasn't. So she went to her GP who informed her she had chlamydia, which can bring about the symptoms of pregnancy. And Michael Martin once had to get himself checked out after he heard an ex-girlfriend had tested positive for the HIV virus.

Neighbours' approach to difficult subjects has always been to increase understanding; whether in the case of Billy's dyslexia or Danni's diabetes, viewers have always been left more informed for watching. And the producers have never shied away from making characters unsympathetic in order to get their message across. For instance, when a Chinese immigrant family, the Lims, moved into number 22 in 1994, Julie Martin was very vocal in her objections. (This

LAUREN CARPENTER

Sarah Vandenbergh

When Brad Willis was catching the surf early one morning in 1993 he caught the eye of a girl riding her horse on the beach. There was an immediate attraction and they stopped and talked before saying goodbye without exchanging names. He didn't know who she was until she rode into Ramsay Street a couple of weeks later and announced she was Lou's daughter. Brad and Lauren were unable to keep their hands off each other, even though he was engaged to Beth. Their affair ruined Beth's wedding day, but once they were allowed to date openly their relationship quickly fizzled out when they realized it was only a physical attraction. Lauren then became involved with a religious cult before returning to her first love of horses. She now trains for an international jockey in Hong Kong.

DEBBIE MARTIN

Marnie Reece-Wilmore

Debbie wasn't one of *Neighbours'* glamour girls, she was just the ordinary girl next door who only did well at school because she worked so hard. However, that didn't stop her dating the dishiest boy in the neighbourhood, Rick Alessi. When Rick won a competition to see Michael Jackson perform in London, Debbie's great-grandmother Helen sneaked her out of the country to enjoy the trip of a lifetime. After Rick, though, Debbie had a harder time with men and when Macca turned her down she became obsessive about her appearance and started dieting. But her self-loathing ran deeper than puppy fat and she became bulimic. Despite the efforts of family and friends to restore her to health, Debbie had to be sent to a residential home for treatment. When she returned to Ramsay Street she had missed out on so much schooling she felt like a dunce. And when her stepmum Julie died, Debbie had never felt less at home in Ramsay Street, so she went to live with her great aunt Rosemary in America.

proved problematical for the actress Julie Mullins, who was treated very badly by a public unable to differentiate fact from fiction. Some taxi drivers even refused to pick her up!) Julie Martin refused to let her daughter Hannah play with the Lims' son and let everyone know she thought the arrival of an Asian family 'lowered the tone' of the neighbourhood. She was quite happy to eat Chinese take-aways, however, and in the end she was forced to apologize for her racism and accept that the Lims were just as nice as anyone else in the street.

Following her split from Brad, Lauren found herself isolated as she had already lost most of her friends for dating him behind Beth's back. Lauren was susceptible at the time, and a local and mysterious group sensed her need for friends. At first the two who befriended her just seemed like friendly folk who were keen for Lauren to become part of their set. Lauren was equally keen for their friendship and allowed them to meet their friends at number 24. Slowly Lauren realized that they were always talking about God, but when they asked her to talk about her faith she had the strength to tell them that she wasn't really a believer and perhaps they didn't have as much in common as she'd originally thought. But they had heard this line before and told her it didn't matter if she didn't love God, because He still loved her and in time she would learn to feel His love. Their support dragged Lauren deeper and deeper into their world, and as she spouted their religious doctrine to her friends and customers in the Coffee Shop, she found herself even more isolated – and therefore in even more need of the cult's friendship.

Lauren became more involved with the cult and started attending meetings regularly. She was keen to go to one particular meeting as she was promised she would meet their leader, but when the leader propositioned her to have sex with him, Lauren came to her senses and fled back into her dad's arms.

Lauren is not the only woman to have had a man try to force himself on her. Gaby Willis thought she had fallen for the perfect guy when she started dating one of her clients from Lassiters, Simon Hunter. He seemed the perfect romantic and told her he wanted to take her away for the weekend to a mountain hideaway – and stay in separate rooms, of course. But when they got there, Simon's character changed and he turned nasty. When he thought he was alone with Gaby he tried to rape her. Gaby managed to make it back to Ramsay Street without Simon, and in one of the soap's most moving scenes tearfully told her mum what had happened. When Doug found out he was livid and he and Brad went to track Simon down to see how he liked a bit of physical intimidation. When Gaby decided she was going to press charges, Simon retorted that he would accuse Doug of assault. Although Doug was more than willing to be convicted if it meant Simon would be too, Gaby knew the chances of a conviction were slight and two court cases would only drag out her misery. So she decided not to prosecute her attacker and focus her energies on getting her life back on track.

Although *Neighbours* has tackled most of modern living's difficult subjects, it has only just touched on homosexuality. When Debbie Martin fell for Doug's boss at the council, Andrew MacKenzie, or Macca as he liked to be called, she did everything she could to make him notice her. And indeed he did, but knowing that he wasn't interested he tried to discourage her in subtle ways. But Debbie failed to take the hint and Macca eventually had to be direct with her and told her he was gay. Debbie was reluctant to believe him, thinking he was just making it up to put her off, and she told everyone in the street. Doug was more perturbed than most – he had to work with the guy every day. But, as Pam pointed out, if he hadn't made a pass at Doug, what was the problem? and even Doug found his mind had been opened a little further. The only other time sexuality has been touched on in *Neighbours* was when Annalise discovered that her long-lost father, Tarquin, was a female impersonator. Although he wasn't gay himself, he spent a lot of time in a gay environment.

WORKING Neighbours

Neighbours had been running for nearly a year before we were introduced to the Lassiters complex when Daphne Lawrence's grandfather, Harry Henderson, bought her the lease on the Coffee Shop as a present. As the neighbours began visiting the establishment for cappuccinos and carrot cake, they started to get to know the rest of the complex.

Jack Lassiter was a familiar face in Erinsborough, but when he fell for Des's ex, Andrea Townsend, and wanted to sell up, Helen's daughter Rosemary saw the complex as an appropriate base for the Australian oper-

ations of the Daniels Corporation. She quickly appointed her nephew Paul Robinson as its head, but the company was still quite small so shared the offices with Shane and Clive's gardening company and Helen's chauffeuring business, Home James.

Also at Lassiters is the hotel, which includes a prestigious restaurant, the Lassiters lake where many a romantic tryst has taken place and The Waterhole pub which was renamed Chez Chez in 1995. Basically, it contained all the ingredients of successful soap: there were enough different locations to bring characters casually into contact with each other and enough jobs on the complex to ensure that characters would legitimately make each other's aquaintance on a regular basis.

The gardening company folded when Clive and Shane left the neighbourhood, although their names stayed etched on the office door for a year or more after they left. Home James became a part-time occupation for Helen, although her services were still intermittently useful. Helen's departure from the office meant there was a spare desk which Paul quickly filled by giving Gail Lewis the job as his second in command.

The Daniels Corporation soon became the Robinson Corporation and Paul's domineering attitude meant he never kept a secretary

ROSEMARY DANIELS

Joy Chambers

Apart from Helen, Rosemary is the only character who has always been in the show, although she only appears intermittently. Rosemary, who is adopted, is the owner of the international organization The Daniels Corporation which owns a majority interest in Lassiters, but bases its operations in New York where she lives. Mostly she returns to Erinsborough to see her mum, to whom she is devoted, but on one occasion returned for her best friend's funeral. In her will, the friend had asked that Rosemary adopt her nine-year-old daughter Tracey. Becoming an instant mum filled Rosemary with horror: she was a businesswoman who didn't want a husband and family but felt she owed it to her friend to try. As it happened, she and Tracey got on like a house on fire. Rosemary is played by Joy Chambers who in real life is married to Reg Grundy who, until recently, owned the company that makes *Neighbours*.

for long. He tried Susan Cole (Fred Mitchell's mistress), who fell in love with him, Zoe Davis, who was too scatty to be useful, Madge, who was promptly moved to The Waterhole and Jane Harris, who was quickly promoted, but managed to hold on to Melanie Pearson, who was too barmy to get a job elsewhere (and after they shared a one-night stand could hold Paul to ransom over a pay rise and job security). And when Melanie left to marry Joe Mangel he gave the job to Gaby Willis, who he eventually promoted to hotel manager.

Paul was not an easy man to work for; he expected no excuses and made no exceptions. Lunch was to take no longer than an hour and there was to be no clocking off before 6 p.m. He made no apologies, but if you worked hard you would be rewarded. Despite his brusque manner, many of his employees found him a very attractive prospect and, unsurprisingly, there were a string of office romances: Susan fell for Paul, Melanie slept with him, Gail married him and Caroline Alessi, who replaced Gail, had an affair with him.

When Paul moved away he left the running of the complex in the hands of his wife's uncle, Benito Alessi, and when Ben moved to Sydney Paul's brother-in-law, Philip Martin, held the reins. But when Paul's corrupt dealings crippled the company in 1994, the Lassiters complex was up for sale.

There was only one person in Erinsborough with anything like the amount of money needed to consider buying Lassiters, and business-minded Gaby Willis managed to persuade Lotto winner Cheryl Stark that this was the money maker of a lifetime – she snapped it up. With one condition; that she be allowed to manage it.

This obviously put then manager Gaby Willis in a compromised position; after all, she was the one with the business know-how, Cheryl only knew how to run a pub. After a few months of being at each other's throats, Cheryl was forced to accept that she was only

CAROLINE ALESSI

Gillian Blakeney

Although it was practically impossible to tell Caroline apart from her twin sister Christina by looking, those who knew them never mistook them for each other. Whereas Chrissie was

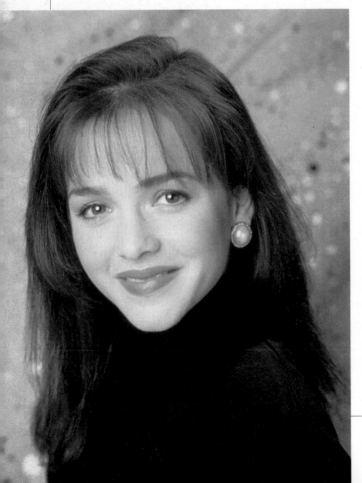

homeloving and maternal, Caroline was ambitious and cunning, and she always felt she had to look out for her 'weaker' sister. The one thing they did share, however, was a way with men, and there was never a shortage of them waiting to take Caroline out. First off, Paul was tempted, but then fell for her sister, and so Caroline dated medical student Adam Willis. She then upset a few people (notably Paul) by dating older man Jim Robinson, but despite several flirtations it wasn't until relief manager Martin Tyrell came to work for Lassiters that she had another romance. But her most explosive liaison was with her brother-in-law Paul, and after just one kiss she realized she couldn't contain her passion and left the next day for a new life in Milan – the Alessi ancestral home – before she ruined her sister's marriage.

GABY WILLIS
Rachel Blakely

When the Willises first moved into number 28 Gaby was studying at a business school in Japan, and as soon as she arrived home it was clear she was going to go far. Her business career began when she made dresses for her friends that were so good she started up a business, which she did by opening the boutique Gabrielle which was successful until her aunt burnt it down by accident. She then hoped to become the manager of The Waterhole, but Paul wanted her as his secretary. Once she started working in the office she became indispensable and was promoted to Paul's assistant, and when Philip left she was promoted again to become the manager. Whatever Gaby set her mind to do, happened. She decided to learn to fly and so she got her pilot's licence, but not before getting pregnant by her instructor. Gaby tried to juggle motherhood and her job at Lassiters, but acknowledged her son Zac needed more attention, so this ambitious woman finally took a less stressful job in Darwin so she could spend more time with her son.

meddling in the office and agreed to let Gaby run the show as long as she left the running of The Waterhole well alone.

The Waterhole has always been a focal point of *Neighbours*, and it has also supplied many of the characters with employment. When Paul told Madge he no longer wanted her as his sec-retary (she refused even to look at the new com-puter) but said he had another position in mind, Madge hoped he was going to give her the housekeeper's position in the hotel. Outraged when her arch rival Mrs Mangel got the job, she was even more affronted when he said he thought The Waterhole would be perfect for **117** her. Me, a barmaid? Madge was slighted but had no other option and, as it turned out, she did make a very good barmaid and bar manager. She had the mouth to both charm and chastize the customers when necessary, she also had the brains and responsibility to tally the float and hire and fire when required.

As well as Madge, Henry, Matt, Glen, Brad, Annalise and Rick all worked in the neighbourhood pub before Cheryl Stark bought it in 1994. And, of course, not only did The Waterhole supply so many with a job, it supplied even more with a drink and the list of regulars consists of just about everyone who ever lived in Ramsay street. Even teetotaler Harold Bishop found his way though the pub's door often enough.

Naturally, The Waterhole has seen its fair share of fights, romances, confrontations and confessions, but the most dramatic chapter in its history came in 1994 when a gas leak in the basement caused a massive explosion which all but demolished the premises. It seemed everyone had escaped without injury until Stephen Gottlieb was discovered. He had lost all movement down one side of his body and was left wheelchair-bound.

The pub was rebuilt and refitted to the specifications of the new owner, Cheryl Stark, who also decided to rename the joint Chez Chez. Before Cheryl won the Lotto jackpot, she had run her own pub and so, despite owning the whole complex, Cheryl only manages the pub and lets the rest of her concern be run for her – she just has the pleasure of spending the profit!

At various times in *Neighbours'* history there have been several other concessions in the Lassiters complex, notably a gift shop run by Christina Alessi and a clothing boutique which Gaby opened, but there has always been a coffee shop which has seen several changes in ownership over the years.

When Daphne died, Harold bought half the lease from her widower, Des, and turned it into a healthfood cafe. Lentils and pulses were a bit too avant-garde for the traditional tastes of

Erinsborough, and Des soon noticed a slump in his half of the profits as Harold had lost all the school trade when he stopped serving chips. Harold was forced to accept that his militant vegetarianism wasn't a going concern and he changed the menu to include plenty of chips and burgers – but he always made sure there was a vegetarian option available. Before Des

left for his new life in Perth, Harold panicked about who his new partner would be as he couldn't afford the other half of the lease himself. Des assured him he had sold to someone he knew Harold would like and told him to wait in the Coffee Shop at a particular time for his new partner to arrive.

When Madge walked in he told her to scarper as he wanted to make a professional impression on the new co-owner, but Madge told him, to his relief, that she was his new partner and between them they owned the lease outright! When Harold died Madge sold, lock stock and barrel, to new neighbour Cathy Alessi who put the Coffee Shop on the map when the Alessi family secret spaghetti sauce created a big enough stir to attract the interest of a food manufacturer. It was her son, Marco, who worked in the shop who made sure everyone knew about it and encouraged his mum to hold out for the highest price. After Cathy had agreed to sign, the food company brought her their mass-produced version of the sauce to taste. It was good, but with all the preservatives they'd had to put in it to give it a cost-effective shelf live, the character of the flavour had been changed. Cathy wanted to pull out of the deal but found that legally she couldn't – at least she was being handsomely paid for her effort. One of the people Cathy employed to work for her was young mum Phoebe Bright, and when Cathy moved to Sydney for her husband's job she was more than happy to leave the running of the shop to Phoebe and her new husband Stephen.

Now that the Coffee Shop was in younger hands it needed a new, trendier, image and part of that meant finding a new name for the place. Everyone had a suggestion to make but it was a near miss with a shark that Brad had while surfing that brought the new name and logo to mind. Brad managed to make it back to shore with his surfboard which had a chunk taken out of it by the shark. The board was promptly hung up outside the shop which was renamed The Hungry Bite.

When the Gottliebs moved on to work in a record store in Anson's Corner, plenty of folk in Ramsay Street had their eye on the lease, but it was Annalise who proved to be the most ambitious. Tired of being treated like a bimbo behind the bar at The Waterhole, she took heart when Cheryl showed confidence in her by letting her cash up and manage staff. She contacted Cathy in Sydney who let her manage The Hungry Bite for her.

But Annalise's new power went to her head and she started bossing around her part-time staff, Rick, Lauren and Kristy, who had to go on strike to make her see the error of her ways. Although Annalise learned to treat her staff a bit better, she still behaved as if she owned the place, so Rick never let her forget that it was actually his mum who owned it.

Annalise's boyfriend, Mark Gottlieb, soon joined the fray when he got sick and tired of the demands of running the Lassiters kitchen. He decided to put his chef's skills to good use designing a more interesting menu for The Hungry Bite while at the same time spending more time with his girlfriend.

Annalise and Mark's reign at the Coffee Shop came to an abrupt halt when Rick decided to jack in school and earn himself some money. He connived behind Annalise's back to take over the running of the establishment. But Rick had neither the maturity nor the experience to run a business – and especially several staff – and the profits took a nose dive. So when Cathy checked up on the Coffee Shop and discovered her own son had ousted the manager she'd appointed, she insisted Rick did something more constructive and asked Annalise and Mark if they'd like to buy the lease from her. They did, and they renamed their business The Holy Roll.

CHERYL STARK

Caroline Gillmer

Cheryl is a big woman in every way, other than the obvious. She's loud, brassy, opinionated, manipulative and demonstrative, but she's also as tough as old boots. After her first husband, Maurie, died, she had to raise their four children single-handedly. Janine, the eldest, joined the navy and she packed her youngest, Danni and Brett, off to boarding school, but Darren slipped through her grasp and gave her no end of grief as he went from detention centre to detention centre. It was, in fact, Darren's association with Michael Martin while they were 'inside' that brought Cheryl to the street where she first met Lou Carpenter. She pursued Lou with vigour until he submitted, and although they now have a daughter together they have never married as a gypsy once told her if she ever married a man in his fifties he'd die! Desperate to tie the knot, Lou found another gypsy who prophesied that if Cheryl were to marry it would be a big success – but if he did it would be a disaster!

MARREID
Neighbours

Nobody likes a good wedding more than the residents of Ramsay Street. Over the years, sixteen couples have said 'I do' and another five have made it to the altar but not to the reception! The first wedding the neighbours celebrated was Paul Robinson's to Max Ramsay's assistant Terri Inglis in 1987, and like many Ramsay Street marriages it didn't last much beyond the honeymoon.

The next couple to tie the knot in style were Des and Daphne. When they eventually exchanged vows the neighbours heaved a huge collective sigh of relief, not because they had been living together for so long, but because it took two weddings for them to end up married!

At the first time of trying, Des was convinced that a girl as beautiful as Daphne would never marry him, so when she was late turning up at the church he shot through, taking his wounded pride with him. What he didn't know, though, was that his bride was being held hostage by an armed robber!

Daphne was travelling to the church with Shane who was keeping an eye out for his little brother, Danny, who was running late doing a job for Clive's gorilla-gram service. So when they saw a man in a monkey suit running down the street, Shane ordered him to get into the car – only to realize when the monkey got

CHARLENE MITCHELL
Kylie Minogue

Played by teen sensation Kylie Minogue, Charlene's popularity helped *Neighbours'* ratings soar. Aside from the actress's fame, it was Charlene's feisty character and relationship with hunk next door, Scott Robinson, that captured viewers' imaginations. Charlene, or Lenny as she liked to be called, was a tomboy who left school as soon as she could to become an apprentice mechanic and was never seen out of her khaki overalls. God help the man who patronizingly called her 'babe' or 'love', because Charlene had a tongue in her head that even Paul Robinson was scared of! But when she couldn't talk her mum into allowing her to live with Scott out of wedlock, Charlene let her actions speak when she married him. It was a teenage triumph over adult interference and Charlene and Scott went on to prove everyone wrong by making their marriage a success. They now live in Brisbane with their son Daniel.

in and took his mask off that it wasn't Danny after all but a pistol-toting bank robber! Des and Daphne's second wedding had no such hiccups, although the honeymoon was cut short when Des put his back out on the first morning. Still, at least Daphne knew her husband wasn't a great romantic before she married him!

Ramsay Street nuptials have come in many different forms, from grand church affairs to simple civil ceremonies in front rooms. One of the most moving was also one of the simplest, when Madge and Max's parents Dan and Edna got hitched fifty years after they should have done. In fact, Edna had always thought she was married, but it turned out she'd been living in sin for half a century when it was revealed Dan had never filed the wedding certificate! After several stormy rows, Edna eventually softened and agreed to make it legal as Scott, Mike and Charlene performed her favourite song at the church service.

It certainly was a more emotionally charged event than the next wedding, which was a decidedly clinical affair. When the Robinsons were invited round to number 22 one night in October 1988 they thought they were going to be served dinner. But as soon as they walked in the door Paul introduced them to a minister who had come to marry him to Gail Lewis. This came as a shock to all concerned as no one even knew they were dating! But the other thing no one knew was that this was a marriage of convenience and that Gail and Paul had signed an extensive – and decidedly unromantic – prenuptial agreement.

Within a year, both Paul's brother Scott and his dad Jim were also to have married and both of them to women they loved. Even though he was only eighteen, Scott was sure the girl for him was next door's Charlene Mitchell. So when their parents refused to let them live to-gether, he proposed, and it was full steam ahead to a fairytale service that caused a bigger stir than a royal wedding.

Henry proudly walked his little sister down the aisle with bridesmaids Lucy and Jane bringing up the rear. He stopped to give her away to Scott, who had chosen Mike Young as his best man. At the time Jason Donovan and Kylie Minogue, who played the teen lovers, were the hottest stars of the teen magazines in Britain, and their wedding was a ratings success. Even the song that accompanied their wedding ('Suddenly' by Angry Anderson) was released to become a top ten hit, while Kylie and Jason themselves were at number one with the duet 'Especially For You'!

Jim's wedding was a more stately affair with no pop songs to accompany the exchanging of vows. His bride was local GP Beverly Marshall, who was to be the first woman in Ramsay Street to refuse to take her husband's name (the other one was Kerry Bishop). After a courtship that involved playing a lot of golf – one of their many shared passions – Jim and Beverly said 'I do' in a service at number 26 which aired on Valentine's Day in Australia. Madge and Harold had also wanted to marry on that most romantic of days, but their neighbours had beaten them to it. However, Jim and Beverly did share the stage with another couple when Paul and Gail made good use of the minister's services by renewing their marriage vows after realizing they loved each other after all.

With all the Robinsons – bar Lucy who was too young, of course – safely paired off, it was time for the Ramsays to get in on the act. Madge finally married her long-time fiancé Harold Bishop in a beautiful church service in 1989 while her son Henry married his beloved Bronwyn Davies in a service off screen in New Zealand. The next family to get the wedding bug was the Mangels, as Nell paired off with

BOUNCER
Bouncer

Possibly the most loved neighbour of all time, Bouncer the Labrador was a dog and a half. Originally the pet of Mike Young, he moved to live with Mrs Mangel when the old sticky beak let the dog see her softer side (and fed him biscuits, of course). He was inherited by Joe and then Toby Mangel, and when they left Hannah Martin took care of him until he went to father a litter and live with Dorothy Burke in the country (in reality the dog died just weeks after he finished filming and was sent more tributes from fans around the world than many of the human stars!). Bouncer was a hero – he even answered the phone and barked to Joe when baby Sky was in trouble – and often had major storylines of his own like the time he was run over and nearly died. But most importantly, he was a loyal and loved friend.

English gent John Worthington and her son, Joe, married Harold's daughter Kerry in a butterfly house after a whirlwind romance.

The next wedding on the order of service is possibly the most unusual one of the lot as it involves dogs and not humans! In a remarkably vivid dream in August 1991, Bouncer the Labrador woofed 'I do' to Clarry McLachlan's sheepdog, Rosie. Well, this is Ramsay Street – and anything can happen in Ramsay Street!

On 19 February 1992, Paul Robinson married himself into the *Neighbours'* history books by getting hitched for a record third time. His bride on this occasion was Christina Alessi and many predicted the wedding on screen would be followed by one in real life between the ac-tors playing the happy couple, Stefan Dennis and Gayle Blakeney. But this ended up being as close as they got to tying the knot since they were soon to split up.

Later that year, the Ramsay Street residents received invitations to yet another wedding and this one was really going to be something to celebrate: Helen Daniels was going to get hitched and they weren't even going to have to get used to calling her another name because she was marrying another Daniels. Michael Daniels to be exact, a long lost cousin of her late husband Bill's. Everyone considered him to be a good match for everyone's favourite granny, but while they were on honeymoon the Robinsons discovered Michael was already

married. Distraught, Helen moved to have their union annulled even though Michael explained that his first wife had been suffering from a mental illness for many years and was now unrecognizable to him.

Ramsay Street's next wedding had a much happier ending, however – especially since the romance had such a gloomy start. Pregnant Phoebe Bright met her future husband Stephen Gottlieb at her dead boyfriend's graveside. Phoebe and Stephen were so well matched that they planned their wedding to take place before the birth of the baby. But the baby was born prematurely and, despite putting the service on hold for a couple of weeks, baby Hope was still too sick to attend her parents' wedding. Or so they thought: in one of *Neighbours'* most moving moments Pam Willis turned up at the service with tiny Hope to see her parents make a lasting commitment to each other.

Joe Mangel notched up his second wedding in the street in 1994 when he married his lodger Melanie Pearson, but not even Paul can beat Brad Willis and Beth Brennan's record of two weddings in one day!

After their first wedding in March 1994 was halted at the altar when Beth realized Brad had been having an affair with her bridesmaid, Lauren Carpenter, the Willises went overboard to make sure their second wedding was a big success. So much so that the reunited lovers felt their big day was being taken away from them and they made plans to marry in a registry office before catching a bus to their new life in Perth. But when they were tracked down on the bus and hauled back to Ramsay Street for their grand wedding, they didn't have the heart to tell their family that they'd already made it legal earlier in the day. And so they put on their formal clothes and said 'I do' for the second time, while resolving to keep their registry office service a private and romantic memory.

In 1995, Mark Gottlieb and Annalise Hartman entered their blot on the 'Abandoned Weddings' copybook behind Des and Daphne, Eileen and Malcolm Clarke, Glen Donnelly and Karen, and Beth and Brad's entries of course. Theirs was to be one of the showiest weddings Erinsborough had ever seen as Annalise was determined to have a picture-book service. That, of course, meant a church wedding and the fact that she hadn't been to church since she was a kid, or lived a particularly Christian life, wasn't going to stop her from making her dream come true.

So the happy couple embarked on a series of meetings with their local minister, but this made Mark feel hypocritical about their actions and he resolved to play a more active part in church life. It was to be Mark's new commitment to the Church that would scupper Annalise's marriage plans, for when he saw her walk down the aisle the hypocrisy was too much for him and he called the wedding off to answer his calling from the clergy.

The last – for the time being – in a long line of Ramsay Street nuptials was Helen Daniels' marriage to philanthropist Reuben White. After Jim and Julie's deaths, Helen responded warmly to the romantic overtures of the sophisticated and urbane gent. But before Reuben could let Helen marry him he had to tell her something that would shock her: he was dying. Nothing could have shaken her love for him, however, and instead of wallowing in misery they decided they would live every day they had together to the full, and progressed with plans for a wedding.

Tragically, it was only a few days after their moving service in which they vowed to stay faithful 'until death us do part', that Reuben died. Helen hung a portrait she had painted of Reuben in number 26 so she could be constantly reminded of their time together.

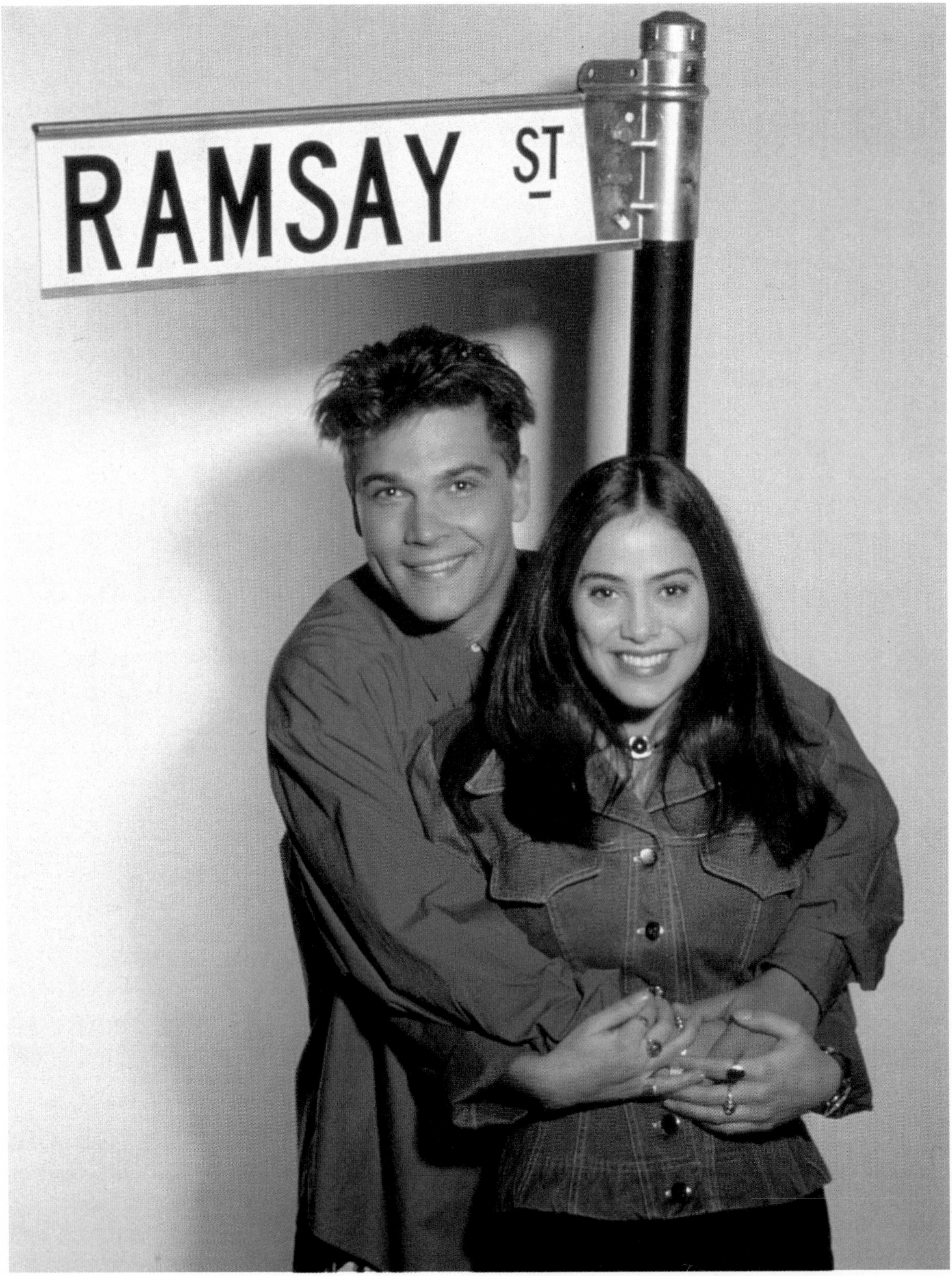
RAMSAY ST